MOVING TOWARD MATURITY
BOOK 5

Growing On

Barry St. Clair

VICTOR BOOKS a division of SP Publications, Inc.
WHEATON, ILLINOIS 60187

Offices also in
Whitby, Ontario, Canada
Amersham-on-the-Hill, Bucks, England

THIS BOOK BELONGS TO

Produced in cooperation with REACH OUT MINISTRIES
120 N. Avondale Road
Avondale Estates, GA
30002

Library of Congress Catalog Card Number 85-62704
ISBN: 0-88207-305-2

Printed in the United States of America
For information, write to: VICTOR BOOKS, P.O. Box 1825, Wheaton, Illinois 60189

CONTENTS

Special Thanks 4
A Word from the Author 5
Purpose 7
Uses for This Book 8
Practical Hints 9
If You're in a Discipleship Family 10
Personal Commitment 11

1 BROKEN HEARTS 12
Seeing hurting people

2 STEP OUT 23
Responding to God's call

3 FIRST THINGS FIRST 33
Praying changes things

4 THE GREATEST THING 44
Loving people

5 GIFTED SUPERNATURALLY 58
Discovering your spiritual gift

6 WITH A TOWEL 70
Serving unselfishly

7 NO LIMITS 81
Giving God's way

8 IN THE DIRT 94
Caring for people

9 MULTIPLY YOUR LIFE 106
Reproducing yourself in others

10 FROM HERE TO THERE 119
Developing a ministry strategy

Bible Memory Cards 129

SPECIAL THANKS

To Debbie Hayes, Nancy Spitler, and Peggy Ward for help in editing this manuscript.

To the Reach Out Ministries office staff for patiently working on this project.

To my wonderful church which ministers to others in a way that makes God smile.

To my wife Carol and my children Scott, Katie, and Jonathan who have loved me and encouraged me to write this book.

To youth workers across America who want to see students ministering to others in Jesus' name.

Barry St. Clair

A WORD FROM THE AUTHOR

Jesus wants to use you to help others. People need a healing touch from Jesus, and that touch comes through us. That's what ministering to others is all about.

Even as you look at the people close around you, you are aware of the deep hurts that people experience. They need someone who says, "I care." Through this book you can learn how to touch people's lives.

Paul said that we are to be equipped "for the works of service" (Ephesians 4:12). As we minister like that, we move toward maturity—"the whole measure of the fullness of Christ. Then we will no longer be infants, tossed back and forth" (Ephesians 4:13-14). As we minister to others that is both how we *go on* and *grow on* in our walk with Jesus!

Giving yourself to others is very hard work—demanding, draining, and tiring. But what satisfaction you feel when a person says, "God has used you to change my life." Then Jesus will be able to say to you, "Well done, good and faithful servant" (Matthew 25:23).

God's desire and my prayer for you is that the things you discover on the following pages will become not just a part of your notes, but also a part of your life. May all that God accomplishes in your life bring honor and glory to Him.

Growing On is the final book in the Moving Toward Maturity series. For best results in your spiritual growth, begin with Book 1 and work your way through all five books. The other books are:

Following Jesus (Book 1)
Spending Time Alone with God (Book 2)
Making Jesus Lord (Book 3)
Giving Away Your Faith (Book 4)

Barry

PURPOSE

This book will help you learn how to see the needs of people all around you and respond to them. It will help you see the need for your ministry and provide you with the motivation and strategy to minister to others. Ministry is another part of discipleship.

A disciple is a learner and a follower. As you learn to make Jesus Lord, you will learn about Jesus Christ and how to become more like Him. When that happens, you will be able to say with the Apostle Paul:

> We Christians have no veil over our faces; we can be mirrors that brightly reflect the glory of the Lord. And as the Spirit of the Lord works within us, we become more and more like Him (2 Corinthians 2:18, TLB).

Before you begin doing the Bible studies in this book, make the commitment to let Jesus Christ bring to completion all He wants to do in your life. Remember: God cares more about what is being developed in your life than about what you write in this book.

USES FOR THIS BOOK

1. **GROUP STUDY** You can use this book as a member of an organized study group (Discipleship Family) led by an adult leader.* Each member of this group signs the commitment sheet, page 11, and agrees to use the book week by week for personal study and growth.

2. **INDIVIDUAL STUDY** You can go through this book on your own, doing one lesson each week for your own spiritual growth.

3. **BUDDY STUDY** You can ask a friend who also wants to grow to join you in a weekly time of studying, sharing, and growing together.

4. **ONE-ON-ONE DISCIPLESHIP** After you have mastered and applied each Bible study in this book to your own life, you can help another person work through his or her own copy of the book.

---

*The Leader's Guide for *Growing On* can be purchased at your local Christian bookstore or from the publisher.

PRACTICAL HINTS

(HOW TO GET THE MOST OUT OF THIS BOOK)

If you want to grow as a Christian, you must get specific with God and apply the Bible to your life. Sometimes that's hard, but this book can help you if you will:

1. Begin each Bible study with prayer.
Ask God to speak to you.

2. Use a study Bible.
Try the *New International Version* or the *New American Standard Bible.*

3. Work through the Bible study.
- Look up the Bible verses.
- Think through the answers.
- Write the answers.
- Jot down any questions that come up.
- Memorize the assigned verse(s). (Use the Bible memory cards in the back of the book. Groups should select a single translation to memorize, in order to recite the verse(s) together.)

4. Keep a Time Alone with God Notebook.
During this study of *Growing On,* you should continue to keep a record of your observations and insights. Your best option is to purchase a set of *Time Alone with God Notebook Inserts* at your local Christian bookstore, from the publisher, or from Reach Out Ministries, and put them in a 5½" x 8½" loose-leaf notebook. Otherwise you will spend a lot of time making copies of daily forms, punching holes, and trying to keep a notebook up to date.

Each set of *Inserts* contains a 10-week supply of the forms you will need during your daily time with God. The *Inserts* can be used to accompany each book in the Moving Toward Maturity series or to continue your daily devotionals when you have completed the series. Your completed Time Alone with God Notebooks will become journals of your spiritual growth and encouragement as you look back and see how God has worked in your life.

5. Apply each Bible study to your life.
The main purpose of these studies is to discover how to grow as a disciple of Jesus Christ. As you do:

- Ask God to show you how to act on what you're learning from His Word.
- Obey Him in your relationships, attitudes, and actions.
- Talk over the results with other Christians who can encourage and advise you.

IF YOU'RE IN A DISCIPLESHIP FAMILY

- *Before* each group meeting, set aside two separate times to work on the assigned Bible study. If possible, complete the whole Bible study during the first time. Then during the second time (the day of or the day before your group meeting), review what you've studied. This time should not be part of your time alone with God each morning. Do not use your time alone with God to work on your lesson.
- *After* you have discussed each Bible study with your Discipleship Family, complete the *Assignment* section of the study during the following week.
- Take your Bible, this book, your Time Alone with God Notebook, and a pen or pencil to every group meeting.

PERSONAL COMMITMENT

I,________________, hereby dedicate myself to the following commitments:

1. To submit myself daily to God and to all that He wants to teach me about growing as a Christian.

2. To attend all weekly group meetings, knowing that through my commitment I will not only have the best opportunity to grow, but that my very presence is an encouragement for the other members.

3. To complete the assignments without fail as they are due each week.

4. To be involved in my local church.

I understand that these commitments are not only to the Lord but to the group and to myself as well. I will do my very best, with God's help, to completely fulfill each one.

Signed ______________________________

BIBLE STUDY

1

BROKEN HEARTS

Seeing hurting people

The girl eating lunch across the table from you says she needs to see you alone after lunch. When the two of you get together she tells you that she's pregnant. She has decided to have an abortion, but she's all torn up inside about it and begins to cry.

How would you feel? Write down your thoughts and emotions as you might experience them in that situation.

People all around you have deep, significant needs, and God wants to give you the desire to meet those needs.

One summer I worked for my dad on a Christmas tree farm. My job was to mow between the trees and trim the trees so that they would grow correctly. In the heat of the summer I spent most of my time sweaty and exhausted. An older man named Mr. Jones worked with me. He was the kind of person who could work steadily 12 hours a day and not get tired. But I worked in frantic spurts and spent most of my time exhausted. That summer I often asked myself, "Why am I doing this?" I wanted to quit. But I kept going because Mr. Jones encouraged me and worked with me. Secondly, I loved and respected the man for whom I worked (my dad). I wanted to do a good job for him.

God desires that our love and respect for Him would motivate us to sweat and get exhausted to meet the needs of hurting people around us.

Jesus speaks directly about this in Matthew 9:35-38. Study this passage of Scripture to see how Jesus views the needs of people. How do you react to people around you?

____

____

These verses tell us that Jesus had *compassion.*

- Compassion means having a broken heart for people in need.
- Compassion means feeling for people. You share in their hurts, their pain, their sorrow.
- Compassion means you care for people so deeply that you cry for them.

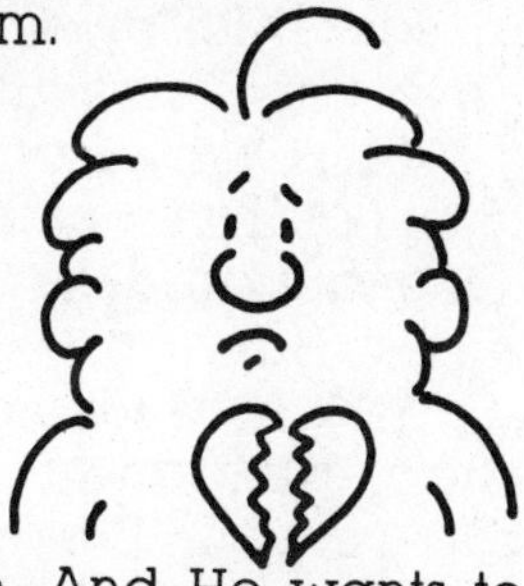

Jesus had compassion. And He wants to express His compassion to others through us. In order for that to happen we must see people through His eyes. He saw the needs of people in three ways (Matthew 9:35-38).

SIZE OF THE NEED

Reread verse 36. What clue tells you how Jesus viewed the size of the need? ______________________

____

A large number of people meant a large number of needs. Let's describe the way that looks in today's world.

Do you realize that every 2.8 seconds there is a new birth? There are 10,300 people born every hour; 247,000 people born every day; 90 million people born every year.

- From Creation until 1850 there were 1 billion people in the world.
- From 1850 until 1930 there were 2 billion people.
- From 1930 until 1960 there were 3 billion people.
- From 1960 until 1975 there were 4 billion people.
- From 1975 until 1980 there were 5 billion people.
- 50 percent of all the people who ever lived are alive today.

(Statistics from Josh McDowell, "Our Challenge"—a message given at the Youth Evangelism Leadership Conference in 1981.) Of the more than 5 billion people in the world, 3 billion have never heard the name of Jesus Christ. One hundred fifty thousand are dying daily without Christ. Have you ever thought about how big the world's needs are? How does what you've read so far in this chapter expand your view of the world's problems? Describe your thoughts and feelings.

____

____

____

SIGNIFICANCE OF THE NEED

Go through verse 36 one more time, looking at how Jesus described the needs of people. Find the three specific phrases He uses. Use a Bible dictionary to find out what these words mean.

1. ______________________________

2. ______________________________

3. ______________________________

As a result of your study, how do you think Jesus wants you to see people's needs?

____

____

Our whole society is full of people as Jesus described them: "harassed and helpless, like sheep without a shepherd." In one hour . . .

- 114 young people will run away from home.
- 28 will give birth to illegitimate children.
- 44 under age 19 will abort babies.
- 1,370 will take some form of drugs.
- 376 will get drunk.
- 570 will experience the trauma of a broken home.
- 456 will be beaten, molested, or abused.
- 58 will attempt suicide—1 will succeed.

(From "Give Me a Reason to Live" TV special, Youth for Christ.)

Whom do you know that is "harassed and helpless, like sheep without a shepherd"? Pick out three people that you see during your lunch period that fit this description. What kinds of problems are they dealing with?

Describe the needs that show up in their attitudes and behavior.

Name	Problems	Needs
1.		
2.		
3.		

Look in Romans 1:25 to discover what Paul says is the root of people's suffering.

Read Romans 1:18-32. List the symptoms of the problems that come from worshiping and serving the creature rather than the Creator.

Paul makes three points in these verses that graphically describe the student culture.

POINT #1: EDUCATION WITHOUT TRUTH (Romans 1:18-23).

Open expression of the Christian faith has been restricted in the schools. If we mention the truth of Jesus Christ on our campuses, it brings tremendous hostility. How do you see that expressing itself on your campus?

____

____

Though we don't know all the results of "education without truth," we do know some. The National Institute of Education estimates that monthly:

- 5,200 junior high and senior high teachers are attacked by their students.
- 282,000 students are assaulted.
- There are 112,000 robberies.

(From National Institute of Education as reported in *Youthletter,* Evangelical Ministries, Inc., Philadelphia, Pennsylvania.)

Because Jesus Christ is not an issue on most campuses today, students are experiencing many deep problems for which He is the answer.

POINT #2: SEX WITHOUT PURITY (Romans 1:24-27).

Sexual permissiveness is rampant on the high school campus (and everywhere) today. On television, 88 percent of all sex takes place outside of marriage. You can see what kind of impact this can make on you and your friends. If you are average, by graduation you will have watched 15,000 hours of television but only attended class 12,000 hours. You will have watched 350,000 commercials that largely use sex to sell their products. ("What TV Does to Kids," *Newsweek.*)

How does TV affect you and your friends?

____

How has "sex without purity" affected students on your campus?

____

____

POINT #3: LIFE WITHOUT GOD (Romans 1:28-32).

This shows up most clearly in the family. Home problems cause tremendous stress among students. Think about how home problems are affecting the people around you. What attitudes and behavior problems do you see in those people?

____

____

General Mills did a study called "Raising Children in a Changing Society." This study concludes that: "Parents are self-oriented, not ready to sacrifice for their children." This selfishness leads to other problems....

- Half the teenagers in America come from more than 10 million single-parent families.
- The average family spends only 38 minutes in meaningful conversation each week.

These problems are causing students to cry out for help. And when they see no answer, many of them commit suicide.

Suicide is at epidemic proportions on the high school campus. Radio speaker and writer Paul Harvey writes of Rod David from Tucumcari, New Mexico—a young man who was admired and successful. This 6′ 3″, 205 lb. athlete was the leading point-getter at a AAA state track meet. Rod was the defensive football player of the year in New Mexico and a top college prospect, yet he turned a shotgun on himself and ended his promising life in his 18th year. Can you imagine why?

Rod David was one of thousands of young people who commit suicide each year. The suicide rate continues to rise. Students who commit suicide feel helpless, much like the people Jesus described as being "harassed and helpless, like sheep without a shepherd." This feeling is rooted in the fact that our society offers no answers to their basic needs.

Students are more ready to hear the solution now than ever before. The intensity of the problems causes them to look just as intensely for solutions. And that's where you come in.

SOLUTION TO THE NEED

What clues for the solution to human needs do you see in Matthew 9:37-38?

Jesus speaks of three solutions to the needs we've discussed.

1. REALIZE THAT JESUS IS THE ULTIMATE ANSWER. In this passage Jesus speaks of being "the Lord" of the harvest. The emptiness of the people around us can only be filled by Jesus, the Lord.

Do you see Jesus as the ultimate answer for problems people are facing? Why or why not?

2. REALIZE THAT GOD NEEDS LABORERS. Jesus speaks of needing laborers for the harvest.

Why, in your opinion, are there so few laborers on the high school campus?

____

____

3. REALIZE THAT YOU ARE PART OF HIS SOLUTION. Jesus speaks of "praying to the Lord of the harvest" to send out those laborers. Every Christian is called to be a laborer. But not all become laborers.

GOD WANTS YOU TO PRAY TO BE A LABORER.

When we pray to be laborers, God will show us the world and people from His perspective. Then we will have compassion—a broken heart—and a desire to let God use us to make a difference in our world.

MAKING IT PERSONAL

During the next 10 weeks you will learn to become a laborer during your lunch period. Here's the way you need to pray to become a laborer who can meet the needs of people at your school:

1. *Recognize the power.* In the midst of all the problems, both in you and in the people around you, where does the power come from to make a difference? Jesus said, "Pray to the Lord of the harvest." The Lord has the power and the authority to change things through you. Let Him be the Lord.

2. *Realize your personal worth.* You are not just "a body" that sits in church or walks around the halls at school. You're not just a person with problems or one who can't do anything about the problems in your world. You are a person with infinite personal worth. Why? Because you are a child of God. That's the highest honor you could possibly receive.

   When a person says, "I work for ______," he is proud of the company he works for. Whom do you work for? You work for Jesus the Lord. There is no higher honor than that.

➩ 3. *Request the burden.* Ask God to break your heart for people. Ask Him to give you compassion. Ask Him to make you able to cry over the needs of people.

➩ 4. *Relate with skill.* God doesn't need an untrained soldier shooting a hole in his foot or a laborer who puts a gash in his leg with a hoe. He needs skilled workers. Ask Him to give you the opportunities to become a laborer.

➩ 5. *Risk the action.* When you see a need, meet it. When you see someone who is hurting, reach out. When you see that someone needs a friend, be one. When you see that someone is discouraged, talk to him. When you see that someone is lonely, love him.

Write down what you need to pray about this week concerning each of these five steps. Focus particularly on people you see during your lunch period. Write down the name of one person and what actions to take to meet one of his needs this week.

Person

Need

Response

Complete this Bible study by memorizing Matthew 9:36-38.

ASSIGNMENT:

1. Have a time alone with God every day this week using the following Bible readings:
   Day 1: 1 Thessalonians 1:1-6
   Day 2: 1 Thessalonians 1:7-10
   Day 3: 1 Thessalonians 2:1-9
   Day 4: 1 Thessalonians 2:10-12
   Day 5: 1 Thessalonians 2:13-16
   Day 6: 1 Thessalonians 2:17-20
   Day 7: 1 Thessalonians 3:1-5

2. Complete *Bible study 2.*

3. Get involved in the group ministry project.

NOTES

BIBLE STUDY

2

STEP OUT

Responding to God's call

You go through the lunch line at school. You pick up a knife, fork, spoon, napkin, and plate. Which is the most essential when it comes to eating? One is *not* more essential than another. Each one serves its own special purpose in eating.

Write down the name of:

- your dad ______________________________
- your pastor ____________________________
- someone you respect in your church __________
- a high school student in your church __________

Which one of these people is the right one to minister to others? Probably you picked your pastor. But is he more essential to minister than the others in your church? No. Each person serves his own special purpose in ministering to others. This exercise points out how little most of us understand about God's call to minister to others.

TWO MISCONCEPTIONS ABOUT GOD'S CALL

MISCONCEPTION #1. *God only calls people to full-time Christian service.* Only the pastor or church workers are called; all the others are "second-class" Christians.

MISCONCEPTION #2. *God calls people to an occupation.* God calls people to be doctors, car salesmen, lawyers, or electricians.

CORRECTING THE TWO MISCONCEPTIONS

In light of these wrong ideas, let's make two corrections that will get us back on the right track concerning God's call.

CORRECTION #1. *The call of God is to know and love Jesus Christ.* Summarize each of the following passages to understand God's call to the people in the New Testament church. Remember that these passages are written to all believers, not just to missionaries and pastors.

Romans 8:30 ______________________________

____

Ephesians 4:1 ____________________________

____

1 Thessalonians 2:11-12 __________________

____

2 Thessalonians 2:13-14 __________________

____

2 Timothy 1:8-9 __________________________

1 Peter 5:10 ______________________________

____

2 Peter 1:3-4 ______________________________

____

Jude 1 ______________________________

____

Revelation 17:14 ______________________________

____

CORRECTION #2. *The call of God is to a particular task.* What does Ephesians 4:12 say about our call?

____

____

By the Holy Spirit, each individual Christian receives his call from God to serve in the church and in the world. You may decide to be a doctor, an electrician, a lawyer, a builder. But God still calls you to be a minister—whatever you do and wherever you are.

In summary, God's first concern is not what job you choose, but that you respond to His call to know and love Him and to minister to others.

What, then, is involved in God's call to minister to others? Read Jeremiah 1. Write down all the insights you discover concerning God's call to Jeremiah.

____

____

Four issues in Jeremiah 1 will help you step out in response to God's call to minister.

ISSUE #1. THE CALL

When God called Jeremiah, He spoke to him! In the same way when He calls us, He speaks to us. How?

____

____

Reread Jeremiah 1:2-4 and underline the four distinct times when God spoke to Jeremiah.

God placed Jeremiah in the world at a strategic time. In the same way God has placed you in the world at a strategic time. Write a paragraph on the circumstances in your world—the circumstances that surround you at school—and why you feel God has placed you in them in His timing.

____

____

God has put you in the right place at the right time, and He calls you to be His person there. Over and over God affirmed His call to Jeremiah. In the same way God will affirm His call to you, especially when you are in the midst of difficulty and discouragement as Jeremiah was. When are some times that you need God to speak to you?

____

____

Again read verse 5. As He did with Jeremiah, God determined before your birth what your call to ministry would be. God has influenced your growth and picked your parents, family, and school so that you could become perfectly prepared to make your contribution to His cause. Now He wants you to discover the calling He has for you. Think of some ways that you have seen God move in your life that have prepared you to make a contribution to His work. Write your thoughts here:

____

____

____

ISSUE #2. THE CONCERN

What excuse does Jeremiah give for not following God's call? (Jeremiah 1:6)

____

Jeremiah felt inadequate. Because of that he had an excuse not to do what God had called him to do. In the same way, our feelings of inadequacy draw out excuses from us about why we can't respond to God's call. What excuses have you used?

All of us feel inadequate to do God's work. Paul expressed it perfectly in 1 Corinthians 2:3. How did he feel?

Now look at Philippians 4:13 and 19 to discover how he overcame his feelings of inadequacy. Write his prescription for overcoming inadequacy here:

Feelings of inadequacy can wipe us out. When I was 26 years old, I was asked to lead the youth work of our entire denomination. I felt overwhelmed and inadequate for three reasons: (1) I was the youngest person they had ever called to work in a major position in our denomination. (2) I didn't have any experience. I had been the youth minister in only one small church, and now they wanted to give me the responsibility for the youth ministry nationwide. (3) I didn't have much confidence in my abilities. They expected me to speak to thousands of young people at one time. I had spoken many times before, but not to that many people. At my first speaking experience, I found myself sandwiched between two dynamic speakers before 18,000 high school students. I felt inadequate! All of us feel this way at one time or another. But inadequacy is not a reason to avoid God's call to minister to others.

ISSUE #3. THE CONFIRMATION

As you read verses 7-9 of Jeremiah 1, determine the three ways Jeremiah had to step out in order to accomplish His special task.

Step 1—Obey What phrase did Jeremiah use in verse 7 to express what God said about obeying Him?

____

In other words, when God says "Jump," our response should be, "How high?" We do whatever He says. If we trust God enough to obey Him, then we can fulfill whatever task He has for us.

Step 2—Don't Be Afraid How did God calm Jeremiah's fears? (verse 8)

____

____

Somehow we *fear* that if we obey God and follow His call, then He is going to send us to be missionaries in Boogaboogaland for the rest of our lives. What we don't realize is that when we fulfill God's call in our lives, whatever it is, we are living life at its very best.

Step 3—Discover God's Anointing According to Jeremiah 1:9, what does it mean to be anointed?

When God anoints us, then we go beyond our strength into His power.

God used two illustrations with Jeremiah to confirm His call to minister. Read verses 11-19. What are these illustrations and what do you think they mean? It may help to look in a Bible commentary.

God uses graphic illustrations today to confirm our call to minister. He has for me.

One afternoon at our Christmas conference the students went out to share their faith. My daughter and I went with them. We prayed that we would have a good experience talking to people about Jesus Christ. The first lady we came to stood outside on the porch of her poverty-stricken home. I told her we would like to talk with her about Jesus Christ if she was interested. She said, "Oh, yes, please come in." I asked if she was a believer and she replied, "I want to be." She told me about her son David who had been on drugs and alcohol. He had beaten his wife and now was divorced. But a year before Jesus had changed his life. He called his mom three days before I arrived and asked her if God had touched her life yet. He said, "I want you to know Jesus and I'm praying that God will send some people by your house over Christmas to talk to you about your relationship to Christ." There we were. We prayed with her and she accepted Christ. That was one of the many strong confirmations of my calling to minister to others.

Don't make the mistake of underestimating your call. When you are anointed by God, He will use you to make a difference in your world. Look at Jeremiah 1:10. How does God describe the effect of Jeremiah's call?

ISSUE #4. THE COST

Very few worthwhile things come without a price. If it hasn't cost you anything, then probably you are not carrying out your call. Remember that Christ gave His life to carry out His call. What is it worth to you?

Read Jeremiah 1:18-19. What does God say to Jeremiah about the cost of carrying out his call?

What do you think it will cost you to carry out your call?

- at home
- with your friends
- at school

COMPARED TO THE JOY OF FULFILLING CHRIST'S CALLING IN YOUR LIFE, THE COST IS NOTHING.

MAKING IT PERSONAL

HOW DO YOU CONFIRM GOD'S CALL?

Go through these seven steps answering each question and asking God to confirm His call on your life.

1. *Pray for direction.* What is God's plan for me?

2. *See the need.* Do I feel a burden for this?

3. *Experience motivation.* Do I have that "eureka" (I've found it!) feeling?

4. *Dream dreams.* Do I have a vision for it?

5. *Share the dream.* Do I talk about it constantly?

6. *Confirm with others.* Do other people agree with me? Do they see me as having the gifts to carry out this calling?

7. *Execute the ministry.* What action do I need to take now?

I know God has called me to ____________________

____

____

____

Complete this Bible study by memorizing Jeremiah 1:7.

ASSIGNMENT:

1. Have a time alone with God every day this week using the following Bible readings:
   Day 1: 1 Thessalonians 3:6-10

Day 2: 1 Thessalonians 3:11-13
Day 3: 1 Thessalonians 4:1-8
Day 4: 1 Thessalonians 4:9-12
Day 5: 1 Thessalonians 4:13-18
Day 6: 1 Thessalonians 5:1-3
Day 7: 1 Thessalonians 5:4-11

2. Work on the group ministry project with the rest of the group.

3. Complete *Bible study 3.*

4. Consider how God can use you specifically to minister to others during your lunch period. Practice this week.

NOTES

3

FIRST THINGS FIRST

Praying changes things

Look around the cafeteria and find one person that you or your youth group has tried to befriend but with whom you have run into a brick wall. List the things that you have tried to do to become friends with that person.

Why do you think what you have done hasn't helped?

Possibly what you have done might have helped a different person with a different set of circumstances. But the bottom line is, no *real* ministry in the lives of others can take place without concentrated, consistent prayer for others. Why?

____

____

All the ministry you can do on your own—without God's specific involvement—ends up like a person who is cramped inside a small box. Without concentrated, consistent prayer for others (intercessory prayer), you're boxed in. When you pray, the sides of the box that hem you in are removed. Then your potential for ministering to others becomes unlimited.

So, before you start ministering to others, you must evaluate. Are you a "person who prays":

- when you get in trouble?
- only during your quiet time and at meals?
- when you hit the sack ("Now I lay me down to sleep . . . ")?

Or are you a "praying person":

- praising God every day?
- knowing that without God you can't do anything of lasting value?
- wanting Jesus Christ to be made known?
- confident in God's ability to change things?

Are you a person who prays, or are you a praying person?

Jeremiah 33:3 gives us one of God's greatest promises about becoming a "praying person."

According to Jeremiah 33:3, how can we see God make a difference in the lives of others through our prayers? Let's look at the three sides of the triangle of that promise.

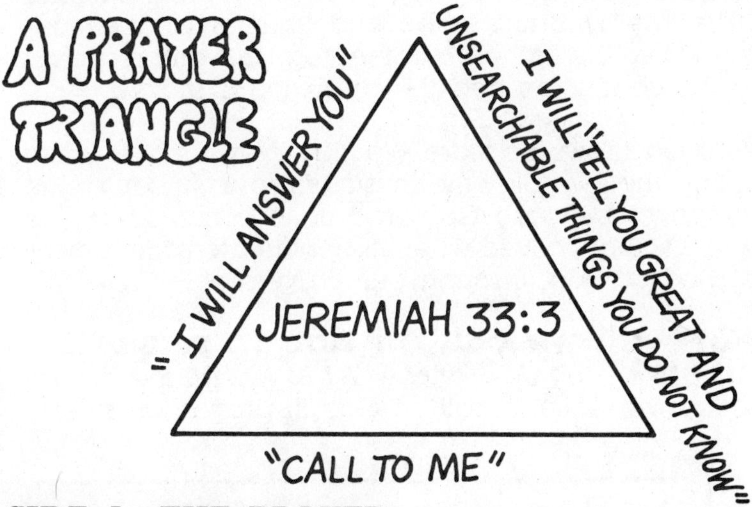

SIDE 1. THE PRAYER
"Call to Me."

Why don't we call on God in prayer for others? It seems that we are short on:

- *Anticipation.* We have no sense of how awesome God is.
- *Desperation.* We are not desperate enough to realize that unless God does it, it won't happen.
- *Ambition.* We are not committed to Jesus Christ and His cause.
- *Conviction.* We say, "I know God can do it, but will He?"

Why do we need to call on God in prayer, especially for others? You might ask, "God knows the answer before we pray, so why pray?"

Let's illustrate why we need to pray for others. An orchestra prepares for a concert. The violinists read the score and learn their parts, as do the trombone players, the trumpeters, and the clarinetists. The conductor knows the score as well. When the time comes for the concert, the house is packed with people waiting in anticipation. Do the musicians think, "We know the music and the conductor knows the music, so let's all go home because there is no sense in playing this"? No! When all the musicians are playing their parts under the direction of the conductor, the music comes alive. The dynamics go beyond just knowing the musical score. The orchestra comes together and responds to the conductor, and the audience is moved.

Yes, God knows the score. We may even think we know it. But when we play the music of prayer, it causes the dynamics between God and us to come alive. The world will be moved when it sees the awesome power of God at work through our prayers.

How can we call on God in prayer for others? Look up Matthew 7:7-8. What three actions should you take to call on God in prayer for others?

1. ______________________________

2. ______________________________

3. ______________________________

Look up each word in a Bible dictionary, and then come up with your own definition:

Word	*Definition*
1. ____________	____________________
	____________________
	____________________
2. ____________	____________________
	____________________

3. ______________ ______________________

The point of these verses is illustrated by a friend of mine whose son turned away from God. Because he was so concerned for his son, this man fasted and prayed until his son turned back to Christ nearly a month later. That is an example of getting serious about calling on God in prayer for others.

SIDE 2. THE PROMISE
"I will answer you."

The Bible is full of promises about asking and receiving. Read John 14—16 and record all the promises in which Jesus says that if we pray, He will answer and give us what we ask.

The big question: What do we have to do for God to fulfill His promises to us? Read John 15:1-8.

God will answer your prayer on the basis of three elements.

ELEMENT #1—THE CONNECTION (vv. 1-4)

These verses talk about a mysterious, vital connection.

Just like branches are connected to the vine, we are connected to Christ. This vital connection between God and us is established through our relationship to Christ.

ELEMENT #2—THE CONDITION (v. 7)

When we have the vital connection, then we will know how God wants us to pray for others. The condition is stated, "*If* you abide in Me, and *if* My Word abides in you." The "abiding" happens as we spend time with God daily. Then we can ask *anything* and it will be given to us. Why? Because what God wants will be what we want.

ELEMENT #3—THE CONCLUSION (v. 8)

The result of this vital connection and meeting God's condition is that we will "bear fruit" in our own lives and will begin to see fruit in the lives of those we pray for. We will begin to see God answer our prayers.

A youth minister told me about a mission trip his church took several months after I spoke there. One night during the trip, he was driving and hit an icy spot. The car flipped over twice as it plummeted down the side of a mountain. To his amazement, except for minor scratches, it seemed that everyone was OK. But they couldn't find a six-year-old girl. Twenty minutes later, they found her pinned under the car; she was blue, not breathing, and crushed. Using CPR, they started her breathing again. They continued CPR for an hour and a half until the ambulance came.

At the hospital they discovered the girl had a broken neck, broken back, collapsed lungs, and a brain hemorrhage. Every 15 minutes the doctor would come out and say, "She's not going to make it, and if she does, she will be a vegetable." The students prayed for her all night.

The next morning they flew the girl to Salt Lake City. When they took her off the plane, she had regained consciousness. At the hospital, doctors discovered *absolutely nothing wrong with her*—no broken bones, no collapsed lungs, no brain damage—nothing wrong at all! And yet, all her injuries had been documented by X rays at the other hospital. God worked through the prayers of those students to heal her. What a miracle!

God's answer may not always be this dramatic. But God's promise to answer our prayers for others will become a reality when we abide in Him.

SIDE 3. THE POTENTIAL
I will "tell you great and unsearchable things you do not know."

What are the limits to our prayers? Look at Matthew 18:18. Do a word study using a Bible dictionary on the words "bound" and "loosed" to discover exactly what this passage means.

____

____

____

The potential in praying for others is unlimited. However, as someone has said, "We cannot expect great answers to prayer unless we offer great prayers for God to answer." One problem is that we are not praying big enough or specifically enough. The New Testament gives two directions that help us to know what our prayer goals are.

GOAL #1—LOVE WITHOUT LIMITS

Rewrite Matthew 22:36-38—the Great Commandment—as your prayer:

____

____

____

One ministry that God has given us is to pray for the church—that it would be a place where people love God and love each other.

The beautiful thing about loving others in prayer is

> that there are really no limits as to how far our love can go. What if you could travel anywhere in the world to anyone in need and stretch forth a loving hand to help that person. Prayer allows you to have such a limitless mission. As far as God can go, either geographically, culturally, physically, or spiritually, prayer can go. Our advocating request actually touches people where they are because God is already there to touch them according to what we ask (David Bryant, *Concerts of Prayer,* Regal).

When we pray we can love people without limits.

GOAL #2—LIFE WITHOUT LIMITS

Rewrite Matthew 28:18-20—the Great Commission—as your prayer:

____

____

____

Another ministry God has given us is to pray that the world would come to know Jesus Christ.

> "WHY PRAY FOR PEANUTS, WHEN GOD WANTS TO GIVE US CONTINENTS?" —DAWSON TROTMAN

God is moving in our world—giving us continents—through the prayers of believers. Let's look at a few examples.

- In East Germany, the German Evangelical Alliance set aside a week of prayer for 650 cities in East Germany. That week 1 million people gathered at 5,000 locations to pray.
- In Poland, a ministry called The Oasis of Light and Life began to pray for revival among Poles. As a result, 80,000 young people became involved in evangelism training, Bible study, and prayer.
- In the Soviet Union, there are millions of Christians

committed to praying in homes.

- Millions have gathered in Seoul, Korea between 4 A.M. and 7 A.M. daily to pray. At one church 15,000 have gathered on Friday nights to pray all night. Twenty thousand prayer cells have met across the city.

Frank Laubach, the famous educator, said, "Prayer is the mightiest force on earth. Enough of us, if we started praying enough, could save the world—if we prayed enough."

MAKING IT PERSONAL

When we pray, we can experience life without limits.

What is a practical way to begin to pray for others? What clues do you find in Matthew 18:19-20?

Let's look at a strategy you can use to pray for others.

THE PARTNERS

Matthew tells us to gather in twos and threes to pray (Matthew 18:20). So let's do it! In the triangle, write your name plus names of two other people you would like to pray with.

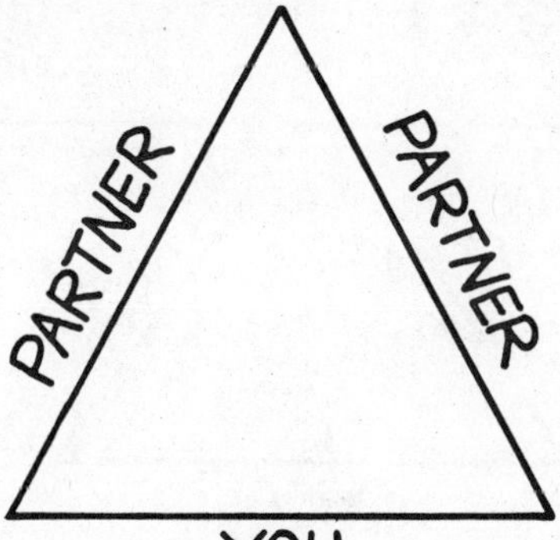

THE PEOPLE

We are told in Romans 10:1 to pray for unbelievers. In the triangle below write the names of three people who need your prayers (preferably nonbelievers).

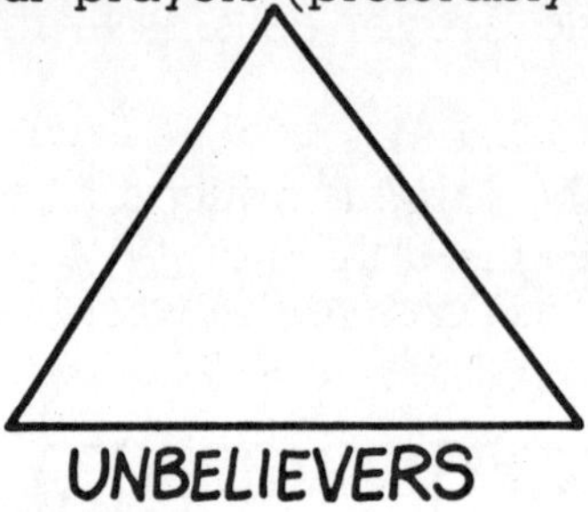

THE POTENTIAL

Even though this strategy is simple, it has great *potential.* Why?

- Because you have two other people praying for you and with you.
- Because as you pray for others, you will touch your school, your nation, and your world.
- Because as each group chooses three non-believers to pray for—that's nine—you will see some of them come to Christ. As this strategy spreads to others in your youth group, just imagine how many people your group will pray for.

In Colossians 1:3-6 we are challenged to pray for the impact of the Gospel on the world. In the triangle below, write one prayer request for your school, your nation, and your world.

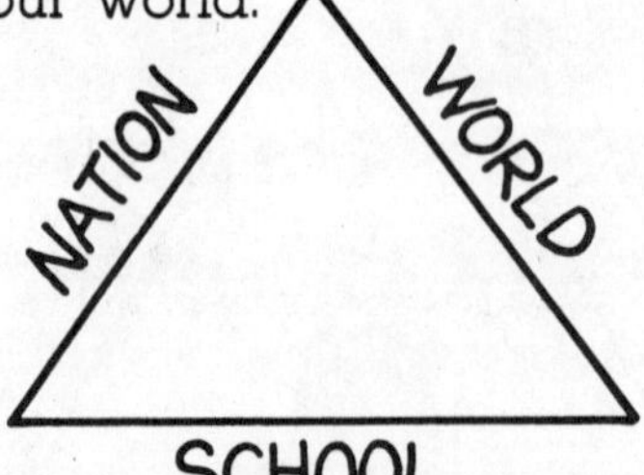

THE PLAN

Spend 30 minutes a week with your two partners praying through this strategy for the rest of this course. Keep notes on what you pray for and the answers you receive.

Complete this Bible study by memorizing Jeremiah 33:3.

ASSIGNMENT:

1. Have a time alone with God every day this week using the following Bible readings:
   Day 1: 1 Thessalonians 5:12-15
   Day 2: 1 Thessalonians 5:16-28
   Day 3: 2 Thessalonians 1:1-5
   Day 4: 2 Thessalonians 1:6-12
   Day 5: 2 Thessalonians 2:1-4
   Day 6: 2 Thessalonians 2:5-12
   Day 7: 2 Thessalonians 2:13-16

2. Complete *Bible study 4.*

3. Participate in the group ministry project.

4. Implement the Prayer Strategy with two partners. Carry this out for the rest of the course. Focus your prayer on God using you during your lunch period.

NOTES

BIBLE STUDY

4

THE GREATEST THING

Loving people

During your lunch period, you look around and see that one of your friends is looking really sad. When you ask if there is anything you can do to help, he pours out the story of his parents getting a divorce. What can you do to express love to your friend?

Ministry is most effective in meaningful relationships. But building a relationship is like having to pass your driving test before you get your license. You've got to know the driver's manual and practice to pass the test. Just as the driver's manual and practice are basic in learning how to drive, love and action are basic in learning how to have relationships.

One of the exciting symbols of people in love is holding hands. It represents a relationship of love. We need to learn how to "hold God's hand" and to hold each other's hands—not in a romantic way, but out of a deep love for one another. When we can love others in this way, we will be able to minister to them. First

Corinthians 13 tells us about that kind of love. Write down the highlights from that chapter below:

In order for us to understand what love *is*, we have to understand what love *is not*.

LOVE IS NOT

First Corinthians addresses the issue of the church splitting up into groups and following different leaders, each competing with the other. Look at 13:1-3.

Paul says to them, "Hey, look. I don't care if you're the greatest, most spectacular person in the world. If you don't have love, you don't have anything." What he might say today is:

- I don't care if you're the greatest debater at your school (speaking in the tongues of men and of angels).
- I don't care if you have the ability to tell everyone in your class what they're going to make on their SAT scores (prophetic powers).
- I don't care if you're the valedictorian (understand all mysteries and all knowledge).
- I don't care if you're the most spiritual person in your youth group (have faith to move mountains).
- I don't even care if you become a martyr (give up all that you have and deliver your body to be burned).

Without love, you can do nothing.

Competition can keep us from having deep, loving relationships with others. We can compete and compete to see who is going to be the best, but that does not matter to God. God wants to develop loving relationships with compassion.

COMPETITION CLASHES WITH COMPASSION

Competition means rivalry—two or more people against each other. They clash; then they compare. (Am I a winner or a loser?)

Not all competition is bad. Healthy competition pushes us to our best. But self-centered competition causes us to want to be first, to get the most attention, to be the most popular—no matter what the cost—no matter who we have to hurt to get there.

COMPETITION CAN HAMPER RELATIONSHIPS

Why? Because you could be concentrating on being "one up" on the other person instead of loving that person. According to 1 Corinthians 13:1-3, there are three results of operating from an attitude of competition. What are they?

1. ______________________________

2. ______________________________

3. ______________________________

Let's look at 1 Corinthians 13 to see what an attitude of competition does to squelch compassion.

COMPETITION CREATES JEALOUSY (v. 4)

The definition of *jealousy:* Deep feelings of dislike toward anyone who has something you wish you could have. It is an attitude of possessiveness—such as wanting somebody else's date. Jealousy squelches compassion because it supposes that God has treated us unfairly and it hurts others.

Are you jealous? Try this test. On a scale of 1 to 10 (10 is most jealous), write how you feel when your best friend:

Gets better grades ____
Is more popular ____
Is better looking ____
Has a better job ____
Has better parents ____
Has nicer things ____

God has a solution for jealousy. Look up Proverbs 27:14 and James 3:16. Write down how God wants you to handle jealousy:

____

____

COMPETITION CREATES BOASTFULNESS

(v. 4)
The definition of *boastfulness:* Being anxious to impress others (for example, spending money you don't have so you can look good). Boasting squelches compassion because it causes us to exaggerate so that we are not telling the truth. It places the focus on us so that it takes the glory away from God.

Are you boastful? Try another test. Rate yourself on a scale of 1 to 10:

Do you try to impress people when you meet them for the first time? ____
Do you feel insecure around important people? ____
Do you exaggerate? ____
Do you crave applause of others? ____

How can you handle the problem of boasting? Look up Galatians 6:14 and find God's solution:

____

____

COMPETITION CREATES ARROGANCE (v. 5)

The definition of *arrogance:* Being bloated with self-conceit and pride. The picture of arrogance is a balloon that someone has blown up until it's about to burst.

Arrogance squelches compassion because it keeps others at a distance—we don't want them to burst our balloon. It makes us big and God small.

Are you arrogant? Take this simple test. Rate yourself on a scale of 1 to 10:

Do you see yourself as superior? ____
Do you wear a mask? ____
Are you prideful? ____
Do you keep your distance in relationships? ____

What is God's solution for arrogance? (1 Peter 5:5-6)

____

____

COMPETITION CREATES RUDENESS (v. 5)

The definition of *rudeness:* Acting in an inconsiderate, unthoughtful, and disrespectful way that causes you to seem obnoxious. For instance, it is rude to tell your girlfriend's mother her dinner tastes like dog food.

Rudeness squelches compassion because it causes us to lose sight of our standard of respect.

Are you rude? Try another test. (Don't be rude and not take the test!) On a scale of 1 to 10, how often would you:

Interrupt others? ____
Talk while others are talking? ____
Make fun of others? ____
Act obnoxious to get attention? ____
Look the other way when someone is talking? ____
Honk at a driver? ____
Get frustrated? ____
Forget to say thank you? ____

Look up Romans 12:10 to discover how God handles rudeness. Write His solution below:

____

____

COMPETITION CREATES SELFISHNESS

(v. 5)

The definition of *selfishness:* Seeking your desires at the expense of God and others. For example, a person gets what he wants sexually when he wants it.

Selfishness squelches compassion because it causes you to watch out for number one. It causes you to fall into the trap of "I'm right and you're wrong."

Are you selfish? Time to take another test. (This is worse than final exams!) Mark on a scale from 1 to 10:

How often do you insist on your own way when someone in your family:

Wants to watch a different TV show? ____
Asks you to get off the phone? ____
Wants to borrow something valuable? ____
Needs help and you have other plans? ____

Look at Philippians 2:3-4 and record God's way of overcoming selfishness:

COMPETITION CREATES IRRITATION (v. 5)

The definition of *irritation:* Becoming frustrated with people. When you get mad and beat up your little brother, for instance, you are irritated.

Irritation squelches compassion because it causes us to live on the edge of being upset. It causes us to get angry.

Are you irritable? Let's take another crazy test. On a scale from 1 to 10, how often:

Do you get angry when things don't go your way? ____
Do you have a "short fuse"? ____
Do you let little things get to you? ____
Do you get frustrated with your family? ____

Ephesians 4:26 tells us how to overcome irritation. Write down God's solution:

COMPETITION CREATES RESENTMENT (v. 5)

The definition of *resentment:* Storing a memory of any wrong done to you (for example, not speaking to someone who didn't invite you to his party). Picture a score sheet recording every time someone does something for you on one side and against you on the other side. When people do things against us, rather than for us, we can build up resentment.

Resentment squelches compassion because it causes us to hold a grudge and causes us to become bitter.

Are you resentful? On a scale from 1 to 10, how often:

Do you feel like people have hurt you? ____
Do you bring up past hurts? ____

To discover how to handle resentment, look up Romans 12:19-21 and record God's solution below.

COMPETITION CREATES REJOICING IN WRONG (v. 6)

The definition of *rejoicing in wrong:* To enjoy hearing about the problems of others. For example, participating in the latest gossip about who broke up with whom is rejoicing in wrong.

Are you "rejoicing in wrong"? Try this *last* test. (Whew!) On a scale from 1 to 10, do you:

Enjoy the juicy stories of the latest break-up? ____
Have negative thoughts about people? ____
Make derogatory comments about others? ____
Find fault with others? ____

In order to discover God's solution to the problem of rejoicing in wrong, look up Ephesians 4:29. What is it?

Because competition is so much a part of our world, everyone is affected by it. Yet we need to remove our attitudes of competition (what love is *not*) in order to replace them with attitudes of compassion (what love *is*). Here are some things to include as you pray for this: Reveal to me how competitive I am. Work the competitive attitude out of me using any means You have to use. Replace my competitiveness with compassion.

LOVE IS

Read 1 Corinthians 13 again. What is this radical, powerful, supernatural love of God like, and how does it affect our relationships?

LOVE IS PATIENT (v. 4)
The definition of *patience:* To have the power not to panic, retaliate, or blame others under difficult circumstances. Without patience, you become short-tempered and frustrated. For example, when your parents do something you don't like, you might kick the bed and pout.

To see how Jesus expressed patience, look at 1 Peter 2:21-23.

____

____

Write one example of when you've been patient.

____

LOVE IS KIND (v. 4)
The definition of *kindness:* To act considerately toward others even when they are not acting that way toward you. Kindness goes further than patience. When a person has patience, he hangs in there. But when he has kindness he becomes aggressive in giving and serving no matter how the other person responds. For example, when your friend spills a Coke on you, you get up and buy him another Coke. Without kindness, you disregard the feelings of others, becoming mean, negative, and critical.

How did Jesus practice kindness? (Luke 6:35-36)

____

____

____

Write down one example of a time you were kind.

LOVE REJOICES IN THE RIGHT (TRUTH) (v. 6)

The definition of *rejoicing in truth:* To experience the joy that comes when your life, purpose, desires, and motives are in line with God's truth.

When a person is loving, he is not mushy or gooey; he is tough. He will not go against God's truth. He will not accept sin. For example, when your best friend starts messing around with sex, you're willing to lay your friendship on the line by confronting him with it.

From John 8:32 and 42-45 determine how God wants you to rejoice in the right:

When have you rejoiced in the right?

LOVE BEARS ALL THINGS (v. 7)

The definition of *bearing all things:* The ability to hang in there in tough circumstances. Our love covers what is irritating in another. That means we never point out the faults or mistakes of another. And it also means handling injury, insult, and disappointment. For example, when your little sister starts getting obnoxious (which could have started on the day she was born), you look beyond it and love her.

Study Matthew 26:36-46 to see how Jesus exhibited this persistent love toward His disciples.

When has your love borne all things?

LOVE BELIEVES ALL THINGS (v. 7)

The definition of *believing:* To have continual confidence in the other person even when that person has let you down. You see the best in people and give them the benefit of the doubt. You believe God will work the situation out even when the other person has done you wrong. For example, when your friend has lied to you several times, you don't give up on him.

Without a believing love, we are suspicious and accuse others, pointing out their faults and judging them. We have a critical attitude that writes people off. Look at Matthew 26:34 and John 21:15-19 to see how Jesus believed all things in His relationship with Peter.

Write one specific example of when you have had to "believe all things" about someone else.

LOVE HOPES ALL THINGS (v. 7)

The definition of *hoping:* To optimistically expect that another person's potential will become a reality. You refuse to accept failure as the final word. You are willing to give a person another chance. For example, if your parents are struggling with their relationship, you can pray for them and continue to "hope all things."

Without hope, you experience pessimism, despair, and depression. You lose hope in God's ability to deal with your situation. In 1 Peter 1:3, Jesus shows the ultimate in hope. What is it and how does it work?

When have you had to "hope all things"?

LOVE ENDURES ALL THINGS (v. 7)

The definition of *endurance:* To hold up under the shock of difficult circumstances so you can turn them into positive experiences.

A person who loves bears up under the shock of persecution, mistreatment, suffering, and even death. He has guts and refuses to be overwhelmed. He is aggressively conquering and overcoming. For example, if your dad and mom get divorced or die, you can keep on going and keep on loving the people around you. Without endurance, we become bitter and try to escape.

Look at Hebrews 12:2 to see the ultimate example of enduring all things. What is it?

When have you had to "endure all things"?

LOVE NEVER ENDS (v. 8)

The definition of *unending love:* To continue to care about another person over the long haul. Love has an eternal quality. A person who loves continues to be committed to the end. Love that never ends has three absolutes: it is permanent (v. 8), complete (v. 12), and supreme (v. 13). Without unending love, we give up, become wishy-washy, and don't follow through on our commitments. Look at John 15:9. What does it tell us about how love never ends?

Write down one specific example of a relationship you want to last forever.

____

____

MAKING IT PERSONAL

Now for the big question: How can you practice love for other people? You may look at all these qualities and realize you don't live up to many of them. But that's not the issue. Jesus is the issue. *Because Jesus lives in you, you have ALL these qualities already.*

Read 1 Corinthians 13 using the word "Jesus" every place the word "love" appears. Because you have Jesus, you have all the love you need. Ask Him right now to begin expressing His love through you.

Now go back to "Love Is Not."
Add the numbers you gave on your ratings for each category. Then put your score for each category in the chart below and divide to come up with your average.

	Total		Average
Jealousy	___	÷ 6 =	___
Boasting	___	÷ 4 =	___
Arrogance	___	÷ 4 =	___
Rudeness	___	÷ 8 =	___
Selfishness	___	÷ 4 =	___
Irritation	___	÷ 4 =	___
Resentment	___	÷ 2 =	___
Rejoicing in wrong	___	÷ 4 =	___

Which one did you average highest in? ___________
That is the area on which you need to work. Spend 30 minutes studying this characteristic in the Bible by looking it up in a concordance or topical Bible. Record your discoveries here.

____

What is the first step you can take toward developing compassion in this area?

Go back to "Love Is." Determine the characteristic you feel is your biggest strength. What is it? ______
Spend a few minutes thanking God for it.

Write down two specific ways that you can express that characteristic of love this week.

Complete this Bible study by memorizing 1 Corinthians 13:4-8a.

ASSIGNMENT:

1. Have a time alone with God every day this week using the following Bible readings:
   Day 1: 2 Thessalonians 3:1-5
   Day 2: 2 Thessalonians 3:6-10
   Day 3: 2 Thessalonians 3:11-18
   Day 4: 1 Timothy 1:1-11
   Day 5: 1 Timothy 1:12-14
   Day 6: 1 Timothy 1:15-17
   Day 7: 1 Timothy 1:18-20

2. Complete *Bible study 5.*

3. Work on the group ministry project.

4. Focus your love on one person during your lunch period every day.

BIBLE STUDY

5

GIFTED SUPERNATURALLY

Discovering your spiritual gift

Look around the cafeteria during your lunch period and pick out the three people you consider most gifted. Who are they? Why do you consider them gifted?

Some people are good athletes, some are real brains, some have all the looks, some have exciting personalities, and some don't seem to have any ability. Abilities come from physical birth. But when you were born spiritually, you became gifted—supernaturally.

Have you ever been asked the question, "What is your spiritual gift?" How did you react to that question? Maybe you reacted in one of these ways:

- "I'm not getting into this because once you start to discuss spiritual gifts, handling snakes can't be too far behind."
- "I play the piano on Sunday mornings."
- "I don't have the foggiest idea."
- "I've been to a couple of seminars and I know this whole subject, so tune me out."

Whatever your answer, think about this: *You can minister to others best* when you know and exercise your spiritual gift. Paul discusses spiritual gifts in Romans 12:1-8. Outline the main points.

____

____

____

____

> SPIRITUAL GIFTS ARE GIVEN TO CHRISTIANS BY THE SUPERNATURAL POWER OF GOD FOR ACCOMPLISHING GOD'S WORK.

The big issue is: How do spiritual gifts affect our lives?

GOD GIVES SPIRITUAL GIFTS AT SALVATION

Look at Romans 12:6—especially the phrase "according to the grace given us." We become Christians by God's grace. Read Ephesians 2:8-9. What does it say about God's grace and salvation?

____

____

We can therefore conclude that:

- grace is a gift.
- grace comes to us through Jesus Christ.
- with Jesus come spiritual gifts.

Every Christian has at least one spiritual gift. What does 1 Peter 4:10 say about one that God has for you?

God wants to give us the very best. A story involving my youngest son illustrates this. One of his friends was having a birthday party, so Jonathan insisted that his mother take him to three stores to find the perfect gift. When he finally settled on "the" gift, he delivered it personally to his friend at the party. That's what God has done for us in Christ. He wants us to have the very best gift possible, and He delivers that gift to us the moment we invite Jesus to come into our lives.

GOD GIVES SUPERNATURAL GIFTS

Read Romans 12:6 again. Circle the word "gifts." In *An Expository Dictionary of New Testament Words* (Revell), W.E. Vine defines *gifts* as God's "endowments upon believers by the operation of the Holy Spirit." What does 1 Corinthians 12:11 say about why these gifts are supernatural?

If these gifts are supernaturally from the Spirit, then . . .

◊ *Spiritual gifts are not natural talents or abilities.* For example, a beautiful singing voice is not a spiritual gift; it is a natural talent. I have a friend who has a beautiful voice. He could sing before he was a Christian, and he can sing since he has become a Christian. He hasn't been given the gift of singing; he has the talent of singing.

As Christians, we don't measure our effectiveness for Christ by our talents and abilities. Whatever we have to offer God *naturally* just isn't enough. Spiritual gifts allow us to tap into the supernatural resources of God.

◊ *We are not meant to seek the gift.* Spiritual gifts are given to us by God. Look back at 1 Corinthians 12:11 and underline the phrase "just as He wills." What do we seek? We seek the Giver of the gifts. As we seek the Giver, He will show us what He has given.

▷ *We are to let God's gifts work powerfully through us.* Ephesians 6:12 says we are in a battle. What kind of battle are we fighting?

____

The passage goes on to talk about the armor we need for this spiritual battle. But what's under the armor? If the soldier is going to win the battle, having the right armor is only part of his equipment. He also needs a powerful, muscular body. Spiritual gifts are the muscles behind our ministry to others. As you use your spiritual gift in the power of the Holy Spirit, you will experience minimum weariness and have maximum effectiveness in ministering to others.

GOD GIVES GIFTS FOR SERVICE

Read Romans 12:6 one more time, underlining the phrase "let him use it." What do you think that phrase means?

____

____

Once you have discovered your spiritual gift, you will have opportunities to learn how to use it for others.

PHASE 1—LEARNING ABOUT SPIRITUAL GIFTS

So how do you find out what your spiritual gift is?

First, let's identify the different spiritual gifts in the New Testament. Paul splits them into three categories. As you read 1 Corinthians 12:4-6, circle the three groups of gifts that Paul mentions:

1. "different kinds of gifts"—grace gifts
2. "different kinds of service"—service gifts

3. "different kinds of working"—working gifts

Each of these three groups of gifts serves a different purpose. Let's take a closer look.

GROUP #1—GRACE GIFTS

These give us *motivation* for ministry. They serve as the basic inner drive which God places in each Christian to build His church. List the grace gifts found in Romans 12:6-8.

MOTIVATIONS

Inward drive to minister

1. ______________________
2. ______________________
3. ______________________
4. ______________________
5. ______________________
6. ______________________
7. ______________________

GROUP #2—SERVICE GIFTS

These *ministries* give us opportunities to serve others within the church. List these gifts found in Ephesians 4:11 and 1 Corinthians 12:27-31:

MINISTRIES

Opportunities to serve

1. ______________________
2. ______________________
3. ______________________
4. ______________________
5. ______________________
6. ______________________
7. ______________________
8. ______________________
9. ______________________
10. ______________________

GROUP #3—WORKING GIFTS

These are the *manifestations* of the gifts as a result of the Holy Spirit working through our lives. They are the outward expression of spiritual gifts. List the working gifts found in 1 Corinthians 12:7-11:

MANIFESTATIONS

Outward expression

1. ____________________ 6. ____________________

2. ____________________ 7. ____________________

3. ____________________ 8. ____________________

4. ____________________ 9. ____________________

5. ____________________ 10. ____________________

To discover your spiritual gift, begin by learning what your motivation gift, or grace gift, is. That gift motivates you to minister to others. Scripture supports the view that each Christian receives only one motivation gift. See if you agree. Look at and summarize these verses:

1 Corinthians 7:7 ____________________

1 Timothy 4:14-15 ____________________

2 Timothy 1:6 ____________________

1 Peter 4:10 ____________________

What conclusion did you draw?

____

____

From each person's *grace gift* (motivation) can come a variety of different *service gifts.* Then, when someone exercises his *service gift* through his ministry, any number of *working gifts* can be manifested. Let's focus on these grace gifts that will motivate your ministry. According to Romans 12:4-8, at least seven gifts fall into the category of grace gifts.

1. Prophecy. A prophet brings messages from God to people, usually revealing ungodly motives and attitudes in others.
2. Serving. A servant demonstrates love by meeting practical needs.
3. Teaching. A teacher researches and validates truth, and helps others see this truth.
4. Encouraging. An encourager stimulates the faith of others.
5. Giving. A giver entrusts resources to others to carry out the ministry.
6. Leadership. A leader coordinates the activities of others to achieve common goals.
7. Mercy. A merciful person identifies with and comforts those who are in distress.

Here's an example of how the different gifts might be expressed. While you are eating lunch, a 9th-grader comes out of the cafeteria line and loses control of his tray. It hits the floor with a tremendous crash, and food flies everywhere. Everyone is hooting and laughing. What would you say?

1. Prophet: "That's what happens when you're not careful."
2. Servant: "Let me help you clean it up."
3. Teacher: "You fell because the tray was too heavy on one side."
4. Encourager: "Next time, walk more slowly and carry it with both hands."
5. Giver: "I'll buy you another lunch."
6. Leader: "Tom, let's clean up—you get the mop and Sue, you get the tray."
7. Merciful person: "Don't feel too bad. It could happen to the best of us."

Which of these seven ways would you respond? The way you responded will give you an idea of what your gift might be.

PHASE 2—DISCOVERING YOUR SPIRITUAL GIFT

These practical hints will help you discover your spiritual gift:

1. Pray. Ask God to show you what your spiritual gift is. What clue does James 4:2 give you about prayer, and how might this relate to your gift?

____

____

2. Study. Make a thorough study of spiritual gifts in the Scripture. According to 1 Corinthians 12:1, what do you need to avoid?

____

For further study, I recommend *Discover Your Spiritual Gift and Use It* by Rick Yohn (Tyndale).

3. Believe. Trust that God has given you a gift. Jesus lives in you, and God has promised a gift to you.

What approach do you need to take to trust God, according to Romans 12:3?

____

____

4. Open up. Open your heart and mind to what the Lord has for you. Don't reject your gift because of your past experience, fear, or preconceived ideas. What are the results of opening up to God, according to Psalm 119:18?

____

____

5. Confirm. Your desires, your experience, and the counsel of others all fit into this discovery process. What does 1 Corinthians 12:11 tell us about how this discovery process works?

____

____

Use these practical steps to confirm your gift:

- Examine your personal desires. What do you enjoy doing most? That is your first clue to what your gift is, but it is not conclusive.
- Experiment with your gift. Don't say, "I don't know what my gift is, so I'm not going to do anything until

God shows me." Try out the gifts you think might be yours.

- Talk to people you respect. Ask your pastor, youth minister, and discipleship group leader what they think your gift is.

6. Respond. With gifts come opportunities to use them. As you to minister to others, you will discover and confirm your gift.

PHASE 3—USING YOUR SPIRITUAL GIFT

How do you serve others with your gift? Read Romans 12:4-5. What clue do you find about how God wants you to use your gift to minister to others?

____

____

____

Balance these two thoughts as you prepare to use your gift to minister to others.

1. Your gift is to *edify the body of Christ.* Remember, God has given us the great commandment to love Him and to love others (Matthew 22:36-38). By showing

love and using your gift, you build up the body.

2. Your gift is to help *evangelize the lost.* Christ has told us to "go and make disciples of all nations" (Matthew 28:19). When you properly use your gift, God can use you to reach the world for Christ.

MAKING IT PERSONAL

1. When you think you know what your gift is, go through the steps of confirmation listed in this chapter.
2. Answer these three practical questions:
   - What questions do I have about spiritual gifts? Refer to Phase #1—Learning about Spiritual Gifts.

   - Which of the six steps do I need to take next in order to discover my gift? Refer to Phase #2—Discovering Your Spiritual Gift.

   - This week, how can I discover more about what my gift is or put my gift into practice? Refer to Phase #3—Using Your Spiritual Gift.

Complete this Bible study by memorizing 1 Corinthians 12:4-6.

ASSIGNMENT:

1. Have a time alone with God every day this week using the following Bible readings:
   Day 1: 1 Timothy 2:1-4
   Day 2: 1 Timothy 2:5-10
   Day 3: 1 Timothy 2:11-15
   Day 4: 1 Timothy 3:1-7
   Day 5: 1 Timothy 3:8-13
   Day 6: 1 Timothy 3:14-16
   Day 7: 1 Timothy 4:1-5

2. Complete *Bible study 6.*

3. Participate in your group ministry project.

4. Try out your spiritual gift during your lunch period this week.

NOTES

BIBLE STUDY

6

WITH A TOWEL

Serving unselfishly

You are eating lunch with your friends and the school nerd worms his way next to you. As soon as he sits down, he starts eating off your tray and making stupid wisecracks. Everyone is embarrassed—including you.

Whom do you know that is like this?

____

How do you keep your cool in a situation like this?

____

____

Your natural response is probably to call this guy a jerk. Instead, Jesus has a better way: serve him The symbol of service is a towel. Towels dry us. And it's no problem to throw a towel on the floor to wipe our feet on. But what about using it to wipe the feet of others? That's what Jesus did.

He gave us the prime example of serving others in John 13:1-17. Write your response to what Jesus did by answering this question: What is Jesus trying to get across to us about serving?

To minister to others we need to learn how to serve them.

From John 13 we can define serving as...

GIVING YOURSELF TO HELP OTHERS.

Most of us do not start with an attitude of serving others. We start by looking out for number one. So how do we begin to change? A towel must be put into action in order to be useful. In the same way, to develop a servant's lifestyle you need to take four steps to exchange selfish attitudes for attitudes of service.

#1—FROM SELFISHNESS TO SERVANTHOOD

Luke 22:24 parallels the passage from John you just read. In this scene the disciples are eating their last meal together. They are arguing about who is going to be the greatest. Study Luke 22:20-24 and note some of their attitudes.

The bottom line is that they were acting selfishly. How selfish we are too!

- We've grown up in the ME generation.
- We're trained from day one to look out for number one.
- Our heroes are people who excel at selfishness.

How can we break out of this cycle of selfishness?

In John 13:1-4, John tells us what motivated Jesus' servant attitude. These same attitudes will break our selfishness and make us servants.

A right relationship to God

What can you discover from verse 1 about Jesus' relationship to God?

____

Jesus was in such close communication with His Father that He knew what His Father was doing and how to respond to Him.

> WE WILL BREAK OUT OF SELFISHNESS
> INTO SERVANTHOOD WHEN WE ARE
> IN CLOSE COMMUNICATION WITH GOD.

◊ A right relationship to people

"He now showed them the full extent of His love" (v. 1). In your mind, how does love relate to serving others?

____

____

What Jesus did in washing His disciples' feet illustrates the same thing that took Him to the Cross: love. He showed the full extent of His love first by washing their feet; later He showed it by dying for them.

> WE WILL BREAK OUT OF SELFISHNESS INTO SERVANTHOOD WHEN WE EXPERIENCE AND EXPRESS THE FULL EXTENT OF GOD'S LOVE.

◊ A right relationship to ourselves

What did Jesus know about Himself? (v. 3)

____

Jesus knew who He was. He had a positive, healthy attitude about Himself.

You would think that since He knew who He was, He would have put Himself on a pedestal and said, "Serve Me." That's probably what I would have done, saying something like this: "I've got it all under control. I've come from God and I'm going to God, so I'm the greatest. Put Me on the throne." Precisely the opposite took place with Jesus. The greatest man who ever lived came as a *servant.*

Only a secure person can serve. Someone who is not secure has to be served in order to boost and protect his ego.

WE WILL BREAK OUT OF SELFISHNESS INTO SERVANTHOOD WHEN WE ARE SECURE IN OURSELVES.

Mark 10:45 says Jesus came not to be served but to serve. He wants that to be our approach as well. The Bible is full of passages that show us how to be a servant. Look up the following passages and apply each one to your responsibility to be a servant.

Matthew 8:9 ______________________________

Matthew 10:24-25 ______________________________

Matthew 16:24 ______________________________

Matthew 24:45-51 ______________________________

Luke 12:35-48 ______________________________

Luke 16:1-13 ______________________________

Luke 17:7-10 ______________________________

#2—FROM TALKING TO WALKING

(John 13:4-5)

The roads of Palestine were not paved. In dry weather these dirt trails were inches deep in dust. In the rain, they became liquid slush, several inches of thick mud. People wore sandals in Jesus' day—soles held on the feet by a few leather straps. There was no protection against the dust and mud on the roads.

It was the custom for the host to provide a servant at the door with a great waterpot to wash the feet of guests as they entered. Sandals were left at the door. If a home did not have a slave, then a guest who arrived early would graciously wash the feet of those who came later.

The day of the Last Supper, none of the disciples would take on that lowly task. All they could think about was how great they were. The room was full of proud hearts and stinking feet. In a few minutes they would pay the price because in New Testament times they laid down at the table, leaning on one elbow on a pad on the floor. One person's feet were stuck in another person's face. It's hard to ignore a face full of dirty feet.

In the midst of all the arrogant conversation, Jesus got up unannounced and pulled off His outer tunic. With a towel, a pitcher, and a pan He began to wash the disciples' feet.

Imagine that you're one of the disciples. How do you think you would have responded to this whole scene?

____

____

____

Jesus gives us some practical clues on how to stop talking about serving and start doing it. Before you look at those steps, describe the "nerd" whose name you wrote down at the beginning of this chapter.

____

____

You can serve that person by using these practical clues:

1. Get out of your comfort zone.

Jesus was eating and enjoying the meal just like everyone else, but when He saw a need, He met it. He "got up from the meal" (v. 4). He was willing to get out of His "comfort zone" and do what needed to be done.

What first step do you need to take to serve the person you described?

____

____

2. Lay aside whatever will hamper you.

Jesus then "took off His outer clothing, and wrapped a towel around His waist" (v. 4). He got *everything* out of the way that would keep Him from serving. He even rid Himself of His robe because it was hampering Him from doing what He needed to do. Without hesitation He laid it aside.

What do you need to lay aside to serve the person you described?

____

____

3. Prepare to serve.

Jesus gathered the equipment He needed to serve His disciples—a towel, a basin, and water (vv. 4-5).

What equipment do you need to serve the person you described?

____

____

4. Get right in the middle of things.

Then He "poured water into a basin and began to wash His disciples' feet" (v. 5). Jesus got right in the middle of those grubby feet.

What do you need to do to get involved with the person you named?

My friend Bill matches his walk with his talk. He serves like that. He's always on the edge of his seat. If the phone rings, he jumps to get it. If someone drops a piece of paper, he moves quickly to pick it up. If the doorbell rings, he answers it. He's always "on edge" to serve.

These suggestions will help you get started with some creative ideas for moving from talking to walking.

- Do little things.
- Guard the reputations of others.
- Be courteous, saying "please" and "thank you."
- Invite people home (after getting your mom's approval).
- Listen.
- Bear the burdens of others.
- Look for ways to serve.
- Make time for people.
- Pray for people.
- Talk about Jesus.

#3—FROM PRIDE TO HUMILITY

(John 13:6-10)

Now the roles are reversed: Jesus has a right to be proud, but He is humble. Peter should be humble, but he is proud. He refuses to let Jesus wash his feet.

PRIDE IS A DISEASE.
IT MAKES EVERYONE SICK BUT THE ONE WHO HAS IT.

Peter expresses pride in two ways as Jesus tries to wash his feet.

Peter is reluctant. "Lord, do You wash my feet?" Defensively, he questions Jesus to keep from receiving what Jesus has to give him.
Peter is resistant. "You shall never wash my feet," he says, as he draws his feet under him to keep Jesus from washing them.

Having humility means we are able to give and receive graciously.

The other morning I walked out of my office at 7 A.M. As I locked the door and turned toward my car, I saw a young woman standing right in front of me in the middle of rush hour traffic with a nightgown, slippers, and a ski jacket on. "I'm so embarrassed," she said. "My truck died after I took my husband to the train station. I hate to ask you this, but would you take me home?" I told her I would be glad to. As we got in my car, she must have apologized 15 times for the way she looked and for asking me to take her home. I could understand why she was embarrassed. But more than that, she had trouble receiving the help I wanted to give her.

#4—FROM FEAR TO FREEDOM (John 13:12-17)

After Jesus had washed His disciples' feet, He sat down again. It was time for some reflection and instruction. "Do you understand what I have done for you?" He asked (v. 12). Their reply was probably, "Sure, You washed our feet. Thanks a lot." But He wanted them to think deeply and to see the significance of His action. Read verses 13-17 to determine the deeper significance of Jesus washing the disciples' feet.

____

____

____

The main point is in verse 15. What does that statement say to you about serving others?

____

____

____

Students often have two reactions to serving.

Reaction #1: "If I serve others, they will take advantage of me. They will walk all over me, and I don't want them to do that."

Reaction #2: "It's one thing to act like a servant sometimes, but it's something else when people treat me like a servant all the time. I'm not sure I want to make this a lifestyle."

If you have one of these reactions, then instead of serving by washing their feet, you will want to:

- Burn their feet with boiling water.
- Freeze their feet with ice cold water.
- Put their feet in a washing machine and hope they get crippled.
- Dry clean their skin off.

We can tell if we are servants by the way we respond when people treat us as servants. We must choose to minister.

MAKING IT PERSONAL

Write down three actions you will take this week to minister to the person you described as a nerd.

1. ____________________

2. ____________________

3. ____________________

Complete this Bible study by memorizing John 13:14-15.

ASSIGNMENT:

1. Have a time alone with God every day this week using the following Bible readings:
   Day 1: 1 Timothy 4:6-8
   Day 2: 1 Timothy 4:9-12
   Day 3: 1 Timothy 4:13-16
   Day 4: 1 Timothy 5:1-8
   Day 5: 1 Timothy 5:9-15
   Day 6: 1 Timothy 5:16-20
   Day 7: 1 Timothy 5:21-25

2. Complete *Bible study 7.*

3. Participate in your group ministry project.

4. Serve the irritating "nerd" in the three ways you decided. Look for ways to serve others as well.

BIBLE STUDY

7

NO LIMITS

Giving God's way

As you eat lunch—munching on mystery meat and corn that tastes like cardboard—a 9th-grader, who comes from a family that doesn't have much money, sits down to talk. While you are talking to him, you find out that he desperately needs $20. How do you respond?

Most people don't want to give. They would rather get. But to minister means giving to others. God wants us to understand giving; it is mentioned 1,552 times in the New Testament alone.

Maybe no one has ever explained giving to you before. But as you look at what the Bible teaches, I hope you will get a fresh perspective on giving. That includes not only giving money, but also time, energy, and resources.

"Give me a hand" is a phrase we use often when we need help. In giving, the issue is: Do I have an open or closed hand to give to others?

Read 2 Corinthians 8 and 9. Write a paragraph on what is happening in these chapters. You may need to look at a Bible commentary to get the whole picture.

Now focus on 2 Corinthians 9:6-8. What do these verses say about giving?

Not having God's perspective means you have a *closed hand.*

"Whoever sows sparingly will also reap sparingly" (v. 6). Here is the picture: A farmer goes out to plant his crop. He has plenty of seed but keeps it in the barn. He only plants a little bit of seed. When the fall harvest comes, he goes out to reap; he gathers up only a little because he has sown only a little.

Many years ago the Chinese farmers lived by the theory that they could eat all their big potatoes and keep the small ones for seed. They did this for some time. They gained a new understanding of the law of life when year after year their potatoes got smaller and smaller—until they were the size of marbles.

A person with a closed hand plants "small potatoes"—saving the big things of life for himself. But God says,

"Do not be deceived: God cannot be mocked. A man reaps what he sows" (Galatians 6:7).

Do you get uptight? Depressed? Frustrated? Worried? Guess what: You've got a serious case of the "gets" instead of the "gives." How do we catch a case of the "gets"?

#1—Misunderstanding the purpose of money

People think money is something that you hoard. But money is simply a medium of exchange. Read Job 1:21. How did Job describe this concept?

___

___

___

#2—The love of money

The lure of the "good life"—new clothes, a new stereo, a new car—never provides us with enough. Why? Because GREED is never satisfied. This poem expresses such a materialistic philosophy.

> Get all you can,
> Can all you get,
> Sit on the can,
> And poison the rest.

What does 1 Timothy 6:9-10 say about the love of money?

___

#3—Keeping up with the Joneses

The relentless ads on TV, in magazines, and on billboards bombard us constantly with the message, "You've got to have it." Then we feel we can't live if we don't have what everyone else has. We read that Jesus speaks to "keeping up with the Joneses" in Luke 12:15. How does He say we should approach the problem?

___

___

#4—Guilt from a lack of honesty

This kind of guilt comes from such dishonesty as cheating in financial matters or lying to ourselves to satisfy material desires. Our tendency is to cheat and lie when we get in a tight financial spot and are about to be embarrassed. James 4:1-3 tells us why. What happens?

#5—Pressure from debts

Debt is owing on a depreciating asset: clothes, car, stereo, or whatever. It means living beyond your means. It's easy to get caught in the credit trap. Read Romans 13:8 to discover what God says about handling debt.

What happens when we violate that principle?

- We get "under the pile." "The rich rule over the poor, and the borrower is servant to the lender" (Proverbs 22:7).
- We become insecure. "If anyone does not provide for his relatives, and especially for his immediate family, he has denied the faith and is worse than an unbeliever" (1 Timothy 5:8).

One person I know got so caught up in materialism that he actually wished his father would die. Then he would inherit money to pay his bills. God does not want you in that position. Read Ecclesiastes 5:13-15 to see what the "grievous evil" of closed-handedness can cause.

Now let's look at God's perspective—*an open hand.*

"The point is this: he who sows sparingly will also reap sparingly, and he who sows bountifully will also reap bountifully. Each one must do as he has made up his mind, not reluctantly or under compulsion, for God loves a cheerful giver" (2 Corinthians 9:6-7, RSV).

#1—Sow bountifully

"He who sows bountifully." Picture the farmer again. This time he goes to the barn and brings out all the seed. He puts his hand in the sack and with an open hand begins to toss the seed out on the ground.

Wealth is like that seed. It shouldn't be stored. God's plan is for us to *give.*

Why are there so many poor, starving people in the world? It's because a few people have too much and won't share it. That is brought about and supported by man's selfishness. There is plenty of food to feed everyone in the world. As God's children,

> GOD WILL GIVE US AS MUCH
> AS HE CAN TRUST US TO GIVE TO OTHERS.

Can God trust you with His resources? Why?

#2—Make a decision

"Each one must do as he has made up his mind." Most people decide to give according to what they can afford. That is *reason giving.* We say, "Let's see, I have

$___, so I will give $___." Instead, we need to operate from *revelation giving;* we need to consult God on how much He wants us to give (Jack Taylor, *God's Miraculous Plan of Economy,* Broadman).

Do you operate from *reason giving* or *revelation giving*? Why?

____

____

#3—Avoid wrong motivation

"Not reluctantly or under compulsion." "Reluctantly" pictures a tightfisted person who doesn't want to part with his money. "Under compulsion" portrays a person who gives because of pressure.

Can you see any wrong motives in the way you have given money in the past? What were they?

____

____

____

#4—Enjoy cheerful giving

"God loves a cheerful giver." The Greek word for cheerful is *hilaros*—from which we get the word hilarious. In Hebrew, the word translated hilarious means "to cause to shine." When we give cheerfully, our faces light up. Being cheerful givers means that we can smile and get a big kick out of giving. After the offering on Sunday, we can laugh all the way home because of what we have given. You may not have that attitude now, but the way to get it is to start giving until you enjoy it. Are you a cheerful giver? How do you know?

____

____

#5—Reap bountifully

"Whoever sows generously will also reap generously." The Bible promises that at harvest time all you have

sown will multiply and come back to you. For example, William Colgate of Colgate toothpaste gave God 10¢ of every dollar he earned as a young man. Later as his business prospered, he gave 20 percent, then 50 percent. After all his children were out of college he gave 100 percent of his income to God.

Reaping bountifully includes more than having a lot of money. It's the treasure of family and friends . . . along with many other things! Jesus said, "Give, and it will be given to you. A good measure, pressed down, shaken together and running over, will be poured into your lap. For with the measure you use, it will be measured to you" (Luke 6:38).

"And God is able to provide you with every blessing in abundance, so that you may always have enough of everything and may provide in abundance for every good work" (2 Corinthians 9:8, RSV).

Why can we have an open-handed approach to giving? Because we are children of the great God who is committed to blessing us. Let's look at 2 Corinthians 9:8 to see how He operates.

#1—God's ability

"And God is able." God can do anything because everything comes from God, everything moves toward God, and everything in between operates by God.

GOD CREATED AND OWNS ALL WEALTH.

How does Psalm 24:1 describe that truth?

____

____

God is the *source* of all wealth.

#2—God's grace

"To provide you with every blessing." God gives to His children out of His vast resources. Look at Romans 8:32 and discover the kind of giver God is.

____

____

God is the *supplier* of all wealth.

#3—God's abundance

"In abundance." God promises that He will give us not only what we need, but more than we need. Look at how He expresses that promise in Ephesians 3:20.

____

____

God is the *surplus* of all wealth.

#4—God's blessing

"So that you may always have enough of everything." God gives out of His abundance to meet our every need. Check out His promise in Philippians 4:19. How does He meet your needs?

God is the *sufficiency* in all wealth.

#5—God's provision

"And may provide in abundance for every good work." God meets not only our needs, but the needs of others through us. Look at how He expressed that in Galatians 6:9-10.

God is the *sustainer* of all wealth.

Several years ago, my wife and I stopped getting a computerized paycheck and we had to trust God for our money. We decided, "We're broke, so let's go all the way." All through our lives we had given 10 percent of our money. Now we decided to give 15 percent. Why not? Ten percent of zero is nothing, and 15 percent of zero is nothing. It was then that we learned the reality of God's ability to provide not only for our needs, but He also uses us to meet the financial needs of others.

MAKING IT PERSONAL

In order to minister to others effectively, we need to take what we have learned about giving and put it into practical steps of action.

Give

The Old Testament Law teaches us to give a tithe—10 percent of our money. And the New Testament says we are to be cheerful givers. If we are not giving 10 percent, we are robbing God. But we need to move beyond that and ask God how much more He wants us to give in order to be cheerful givers. What percentage of your money are you giving to God now? What percentage of your money does He want you to give?

____

Get out of debt

Proverbs 22:7 tells us why we need to get out of debt and stay out. What does it say?

____

If you're in debt, get out. If you can't get out of debt by paying off your bills in one month, then you need to get counsel from your parents, youth minister, or discipleship group leader on how to get out of debt.

Are you in debt? ___ How much? ___ Can you get out in a month? ___

What steps are you going to take to get out of debt?

____

____

Lend

When we lend money, we expect people to repay—often with interest. But look at what Jesus says about that as recorded in Matthew 5:42.

____

____

The problem with lending and expecting a return is that:

- We get people obligated to us.
- We become resentful or bitter when they don't repay us.
- We harm our friendship.

So how do we handle it when someone needs to borrow money from us and we want to help him? WE GIVE THE MONEY NOT EXPECTING IT TO BE RETURNED.

Whom have you loaned money to? ____________ Do you expect it back? ____________ Is this causing you to resent that person? ____ If so, you need to have a heart-to-heart talk with him. If a conversation is necessary, record the results below.

____

____

Budget

God has made you a "steward" of the money He has given you. Look in a Bible dictionary to discover what "steward" means.

____

____

To be a good steward of God's money you need to answer these questions before each purchase. Do I need this item? Do I have the money to pay cash? Is it high on my priority list? Have I shopped for the best buy? Did I ask God to either confirm this purchase or remove my desire for it?

To learn to spend your money wisely, work out your budget including 10 percent of your income for tithe, at least 5 percent for additional giving, and 5 percent for savings.

Save

What does Proverbs 13:22 say about saving money?

____

____

If we save, we will have more money. Then when needs arise, we can meet more of them because we have more money to give away.

WE HAVE THE PRIVILEGE OF GIVING
TO THE GREATEST CAUSE IN THE WORLD—
THE CAUSE OF JESUS CHRIST.

Complete this Bible study by memorizing 2 Corinthians 9:6-7.

ASSIGNMENT:

1. Have a time alone with God every day this week using the following Bible readings:
   Day 1: 1 Timothy 6:1-2
   Day 2: 1 Timothy 6:3-10
   Day 3: 1 Timothy 6:11-16
   Day 4: 1 Timothy 6:17-21
   Day 5: 2 Timothy 1:1-7
   Day 6: 2 Timothy 1:8-12
   Day 7: 2 Timothy 1:13-18

2. Complete *Bible study 8.*

3. Work on your group ministry project.

4. Make a realistic and workable budget.

NOTES

IN THE DIRT

Caring for people

Imagine . . . lunch is over, and you're trying to help the person next to you by taking his tray and emptying it for him. When you pick it up, he moves his arm and flips the remains of the corn dog and french fries with catsup and mustard all over the front of your sweater. Which of the following responses would you make?

- ☐ "I'll never help him again."
- ☐ "It doesn't pay to help people."
- ☐ "I'm really ticked about my sweater."
- ☐ "That's just a part of helping people."

GOD WANTS US TO GET DIRTY
CARING FOR OTHER PEOPLE.

When we minister to others we can count on getting dirty. When people hurt, they want to know we care. Charles Schulz's cartoon character Linus plucked petals from a daisy while reciting, "Does anybody up there (out there, down there) care?"

And we show them we care by "grubbing it out in their dirt."

Luke tells a marvelous story about getting dirty while caring for other people. Read Luke 10:25-37, and record the main point of these verses:

____

____

____

Who is your neighbor—is it friends at school, the girl in English class, the weird kid with the locker next to yours, or the old man who lives down the street? Jesus, the master storyteller, responded to that question with the Parable of the Good Samaritan, which you just read. Let's review the script.

ACT I: THE PAIN (v. 30)

A man was traveling from Jerusalem to Jericho alone. It was a very dangerous road to travel. On the way, this man ran into some trouble. What happened to him?

____

____

People all around us are just like that. They may look like us and dress like we do, but inside they are stripped, beaten, and half-dead. Do you know any people who have been . . .

- "stripped"—of their parents, their friends, or their relationship to God? Who? ____________ Describe them:

____

____

◊ "beaten" black and blue—on their body or in their feelings? Who? ____________________ Describe them:

____

____

◊ "left half-dead"—assaulted by the enemy in a way that causes self-hate, depression, or thoughts of suicide? Who? ____________________ Describe them:

____

____

ACT II: THE DISDAIN (vv. 31-32)

Many people disdain getting dirty and have therefore become insensitive to people's needs.

Two of the characters in the Parable of the Good Samaritan are like that.

The Priest

He saw this man on the side of the road and still passed by. Why? He knew that if he touched this man he could become "ceremonially unclean." The priest was not sure if the man was dead or not. But Jewish Law said that if a person touched a dead man, then that person would be unclean for seven days (Numbers 19:11). That meant he would not be a good Jew and other Jews would look down on him. Because of that, he passed on by. The point: Getting dirty for others may mean risking your reputation with your friends.

Would your church friends begin to question your reputation if you started hanging around with someone who was in trouble with drugs—even though you knew God led you to minister to him?

____

____

Would you get dirty to help someone else if it might mean losing your reputation with your friends? Why or why not?

The Levite

The Levite wanted to protect himself. In those days, robbers used decoys. One robber would act like a wounded man. Then when an unsuspecting traveler stopped by, the other one would rush out and rob him. Because of this, these religious men had a motto: "Safety first." Protect yourself and take no risks when it comes to helping someone else. The point: Getting dirty for others may mean taking risks.

But let's not condemn these men too quickly. We get caught in these traps as well. How often have you passed by a person who was out of gas on the side of the road? Or a person at school who had just dropped his books? Would you "get dirty" for someone else if it meant taking a risk? Why or why not?

ACT III: THE STAIN (vv. 33-35)

Jews hated Samaritans so much that when Jesus mentioned the name "Samaritan" it made the lawyer bristle. Jews didn't want to have anything to do with Samaritans. They would go to any lengths to avoid Samaria when they were traveling from Judea to Galilee (a straight shot through Samaria). To the Jews, the Samaritan was definitely the villain and not the hero. So when Jesus used a Samaritan in His illustration, His disciples knew He needed a course in "How to Win Friends and Influence People."

So, the Samaritan came along and saw the same thing the Jewish priest and the Levite saw. But he stopped to help. Here was a man who was not afraid to get dirty for someone else. Name one person who has gotten dirty for you. What does that person mean to you?

Name one person who would get you dirty if you tried to minister to him.

____

Now let's learn from the Good Samaritan how we can get dirty. He did it by...

1. Going—"as he traveled" (v. 32). He was moving along in his daily routine. When Jesus tells us to "go" in Matthew 28:19-20, what does He tell us to do along the way?

____

____

List the places you go every day where you can minister to the person you mentioned above.

____

____

2. Loving—"he took pity on him" (v. 33). This is the turning point in the story. It's the difference between the Samaritan and the other two men. The Samaritan had a compassion for people that sprang from an inner desire to please God; all the others had were external religious trappings.

We have that same inner desire because Christ lives in us. From John 15:9-17, discover how that compassion is supposed to work in our lives.

____

____

____

____

IT'S EASY TO GET CHRISTIANITY
INTO OUR HEADS, BUT IT'S TOUGH TO MAKE
THE JOURNEY INTO OUR HEARTS.

What difficulties are you having in letting your compassion flow freely toward others?

____

____

What is one way you can show compassion to the person whose name you wrote on page 98?

____

3. Coming—"went to him" (v. 34). The Samaritan overlooked the risks. He skipped the question, "Will he take advantage of me?" He dodged the bullet of apathy and got involved.

Jesus got involved as well, as recorded in Luke 8:40-48. Read that story and write down how Jesus responded to the situation.

____

____

In order to get dirty we have to jump in with both feet and GO FOR IT! What one way can you get involved with the person named on page 98?

____

____

4. Touching—"bandaged his wounds, pouring on oil and wine" (v. 34). In order to bind the man's wounds he had to touch him. Imagine what the beaten man looked like. Describe him:

____

____

What do you think helping him did to the Samaritan's clean robe? ______________________________

Jesus wants us to touch other people like He did. Look at one example of how Jesus touched others in Luke 5:12-16. What did it involve?

____

____

____

Sometimes all it takes is a touch—a hug, a pat on the back—to make the difference. In what way can you touch the person you mentioned before in order to minister to him?

____

____

____

5. Sacrificing—"then he put the man on his own donkey" (v. 34). When he sat the beaten man on his own beast, that meant the Samaritan had to walk. He didn't say, "I can't do this because I'll get blisters on my heels." The Samaritan was willing to sacrifice in order to meet the need.

Read Jesus' statement in Luke 9:23-25. What are the three steps involved in sacrifice?

____

____

____

What is one specific sacrifice you can make in order to minister to the person whose name you mentioned?

____

____

6. Being inconvenienced—"took him to an inn" (v. 34). The Samaritan inconvenienced himself—he went out of his way. He probably hadn't planned to go to that inn before; but he went in order to take care of his neighbor.

How far does Jesus say we need to be willing to go to minister to others? See Matthew 5:41.

____

____

What can you do to go out of your way for the person you mentioned?

____

____

7. Caring—"and took care of him" (v. 34). We know that the Samaritan spent the night because the Bible says "the next day" (v. 35). His time was important, but he was willing to give it. This is one way we know that the Samaritan took care of him.

Time is our most precious possession, but we need to give it to meet the needs of others. Look at how Paul says we need to use our time in Ephesians 5:15-16:

____

____

How can you use your time to minister to the person whose name you mentioned?

____

____

8. Giving—"he took out two silver coins" (v. 35). These coins were denarii. When he paid them to the innkeeper they were worth two months' board. The Samaritan was willing to give his money in order to minister to his neighbor.

Jesus tells us what will happen to us when we give like that (Luke 6:38). Summarize what He says below.

____

____

Name one specific way you can give your money to meet the needs of the person whose name you mentioned.

____

____

9. Continuing—"Look after him, and when I return" (v. 35). The Samaritan followed through. He kept on looking after the man. He completed the project that he started.

The Apostle Paul tells us what our response needs to be toward following through with people even when we don't feel like it. What does he say in Galatians 6:9-10?

____

____

Name one way you can follow through in caring for the person whose name you mentioned.

____

____

10. Expending—"I will reimburse you for any extra expense you may have" (v. 35). The Samaritan was saying, "If there is any other expense, I will take care of it." He went beyond the minimum requirement in helping his neighbor.

First John 3:17-18 gives us the reason for going beyond the minimum requirement and the way to go about it. What does it say?

____

____

How can you go beyond the minimum requirement in helping the person whose name you mentioned?

____

____

____

In our church an 18-year-old girl has had several "Good Samaritans" take care of her. When she was 8 years old, her parents abandoned her in a big city. For the next five years she was homeless and lived on the streets. This led to her involvement with drugs and eventual addiction to heroin. When she was 13, the state took custody of her and placed her in a foster home. For several years she was moved from one foster home to another, often living on the streets. This lasted five years.

One day, she met a guy in our church named Cliff. Cliff invited her to go to church with him. She didn't want to because she was afraid of what people would think of her. Finally, after much encouragement, she went. To her surprise, people reached out and accepted her.

She soon saw her need for Christ and committed her life to Him. As a result, she overcame her drug addiction. Some of the girls in our church bought her new clothes. One girl, who had previously used drugs, took her under her wing. One of the men in our church is guiding her as she grows in her faith in Jesus Christ. Others are teaching her to read and write. To bring the story full circle, this young lady has led her first person to Christ.

She is no different than the man on the side of the road

in the Parable of the Good Samaritan. And she is no different than people in your school who need you to minister to them.

ACT IV: THE GAIN

When we have a lifestyle of getting dirty for God, then we will reap the benefits that come with it. Jesus tells us what those benefits are. Read Matthew 25:31-40 and write down what He says will happen to us on that day of judgment.

____

____

____

____

As we reflect on all the things the Samaritan did, it's obvious that he sacrificed a great deal. Because of this he was never quite the same. He had a dirty robe and he was a few dollars poorer, but he had the inexpressible satisfaction of being part of God's solution to someone's need. We can have that same satisfaction in our lives as we learn to get dirty for God.

Complete this Bible study by memorizing Matthew 22:37-39.

MAKING IT PERSONAL

Follow through on each step in order to get dirty by helping the person whose name you wrote down.

ASSIGNMENT:

1. Have a time alone with God every day this week using the following Bible readings:
   Day 1: 2 Timothy 2:1-7
   Day 2: 2 Timothy 2:8-13
   Day 3: 2 Timothy 2:14-19
   Day 4: 2 Timothy 2:20-21
   Day 5: 2 Timothy 2:22-26
   Day 6: 2 Timothy 3:1-5
   Day 7: 2 Timothy 3:6-9

2. Complete *Bible study 9.*

3. Participate in your group ministry project.

NOTES

BIBLE STUDY

9

MULTIPLY YOUR LIFE

Reproducing yourself in others

Look around as you eat in the cafeteria this week. Who has a real desire to grow as a Christian? Write that person's name here.____________________

Now describe everything you know about that person.

Do you think that person would meet regularly with you so you could help him grow?__________

You may have responded:

- ☐ He wouldn't want to meet with me.
- ☐ I feel so inadequate.
- ☐ I wouldn't know where to start.
- ☐ What would I tell him?

Most people feel inadequate, but God wants to use you.

Douglas Hyde was a Communist before he committed his life to Christ. In his book *Dedication and Leadership* (Harper & Row) he tells of a man who came to him after a lecture one night and said, "Ca . . . ca . . . ca . . . can I become a Co . . . Co . . . Communist?" In all his career Hyde had never seen such an unlikely person want to become a Communist. He knew the unbreakable rule of the Communist Party—"Every person a potential Communist, every person a potential leader in Communism." But this man just did not seem to fill the bill. Almost speechless, Hyde told him to come back the next week for an answer.

During the week Hyde met with his superiors. They told him: "You know the unbreakable rule. This man can become a Communist." Hyde protested about how bad off this man was, but his superiors insisted.

The next week he gave his lecture. Afterward the man came to him again: "Ca . . . ca . . . can I become a Co . . . Co . . . Communist?" Douglas Hyde told him that he could. That man joined the Communist Party and moved up through the ranks until he headed the world distribution of Communist literature.

Every person who has the *desire* can become a Christian. And every Christian who has the *desire* can be a leader of others. You have demonstrated that kind of desire by working through the first four courses of *Moving Toward Maturity*. God has used your leader in this process to discipline you in your walk with Christ. What your leader has done with you, the Bible calls "making disciples."

Think about how being discipled has helped you grow strong in your relationship to Jesus Christ:

____

____

____

____

____

From what you have experienced in your own life, how would you describe disciple-making?

____

____

____

____

In Jesus' last command to His disciples He gives this clear direction: "make disciples" (Matthew 28:19). Here is one way to define disciple-making:

> One maturing believer
> Reproducing other maturing believers
> To the degree that they are able to
> Reproduce maturing believers
> Through the local church.

Using this definition, how can you become a disciple-maker? Let's look at it like this:

Disciple-making is like building a homecoming float. You need certain building materials to make the float a winner: lumber, nails, chicken wire, tissues, and other items. If we are going to be disciple-makers, then we have to have the essential supplies. Those supplies are identified in 2 Timothy 2:1-2. See if you can discover from these two verses the essential materials for making disciples:

____

____

____

____

Now let's see how your list of discipling materials compares to the list below.

#1. STAY CLOSE TO CHRIST. Focus on the phrase "be strong in the grace that is in Christ Jesus"

(v. 1). Using a word study book, discover what that phrase means.

A high school student got a summer job painting stripes down the highway. With great enthusiasm he painted 5 miles of stripes on his first day. The next day he painted 2 miles, the next day three fourths of a mile, the next day 200 yards, and the next day he painted 10 feet. The supervisor called him in, telling him he set a company record for painting stripes on the first day, but on the last day he had done worse than anyone on the job. The supervisor asked him what the problem was. He replied, "I just kept getting farther and farther away from the bucket."

Unless we stay close to the bucket, we will lose our effectiveness too. Our "bucket" is Jesus, and if we don't stay close to Him, we will lose our ability to operate in the Spirit and to make an impact on the lives of others.

Read John 15:1-8. What is involved in staying close to Christ?

THE POINT: STAY CLOSE TO CHRIST. Your ability to disciple others does not depend on your great personality, your creativity, your skills, or your good looks; it depends on staying close to Jesus Christ.

What is the main thing you need to work on in order to stay close to Christ?

#2. MAKE A FRIEND. Read 2 Timothy 2:2 and circle the words "you" and "me."

Paul and Timothy had a close friendship. What does 2 Timothy 1 tell you about the depth of their friendship?

After spending some time with my friend Lee, I discovered he was confused about his relationship with God. We started getting together every week. As a result, he accepted Christ. After that we spent even more time together. Through our friendship, he became a bold witness on his campus. Since that time he has become the editor of the largest Christian newspaper for college students in America. He called me last Thanksgiving to thank me for the time I invested in him to help him know Jesus and grow in Him. From that experience I learned that true discipleship is built on close friendships that center around our relationships to Christ.

From 1 Thessalonians 2:7-8, what do we learn about the kind of friendships we need to build in making disciples?

THE POINT: DEVELOP A FRIENDSHIP WITH YOUR DISCIPLE. With whom do you have that kind of friendship? Reflect on how you became such close friends. You can use these ideas in building other friendships with potential disciples.

#3. REFLECT JESUS' CHARACTER. Go back to 2 Timothy 2:2 and underline the word "commit" or "entrust."

One way to look at this word is that it is like putting something in a safety-deposit box. That's where people keep their valuable deeds, stocks, and bonds. When they go to the bank to open the safety-deposit box, they can't open it with their key only. Two keys are necessary. The bank's key and renter's key turn together to open the door to all the valuable items.

"Commit" means two people related to each other in partnership with the Spirit of God. They open up and discover the riches of Christ's character in each other, then reflect the character of Jesus Christ through their lives by attitudes, thoughts, actions, and habits.

Paul tells us how that works for us (2 Corinthians 3:18). What does he say?

____

____

Some of the riches Paul passed along to his friend Timothy—and which you will want to pass along—are found in 2 Timothy 3:10-11. What are they?

____

THE POINT: REFLECT THE CHARACTER OF CHRIST. In what specific ways do you think you reflect Christ?

____

____

#4. BE REAL WITH OTHERS. Paul speaks of reflecting Christ "in the presence of many witnesses' (2 Timothy 2:2). By that he means *be real.* Have you ever thought, "To disciple someone, I need to be super-spiritual and close to perfect, with everything absolutely cool in my life"? That's wrong. Again and again, experience shows that people respond best to people who are "real."

Kent, a student I was discipling, came over to help me move some furniture. Behind the first couch were Tinker-toys, moldy raisins, building blocks, and other assorted junk. He looked embarrassed. Then we moved a hide-a-bed. When we folded it out a big glob of stuffing came out. He blushed and the look on his face said, "Cheap couch." The last couch measured 86 inches long and 38 inches high. We had to get it through a door 79 inches high and 29 inches wide. When we started through the door, Kent pinched my fingers. I yelled at him. I rammed his fingers into the wall. For two hours we scraped the paint off the walls and the doorway pushing and pulling, sweating, and getting exhausted—totally frustrated. We never did get the couch through the door.

He saw me in a real-life situation. No longer was I on a spiritual pedestal. But instead of respecting me less, his seeing my weaknesses drew us closer.

Look up 2 Corinthians 12:9. What did one of the greatest disciplers say about how he handled his weaknesses?

____

____

____

In 1 Corinthians 2:3-5 we are told how and why we can be real as we disciple others. What do these verses say?

____

____

____

When we're open about our weaknesses it helps others keep their eyes on Jesus.

THE POINT: BE YOURSELF WITH OTHER PEOPLE. When do you have the most difficulty being open and transparent? Why?

#5. FIND THE RIGHT DISCIPLE. Go back to 2 Timothy 2:2 and circle the words "reliable men" or "faithful men." Look up that phrase in a word study book and write the definition.

The desires of a faithful man are expressed in Psalm 42:1-2 and Psalm 63:1. What are they?

How does Paul describe his disciples in 1 Thessalonians 1:3?

A faithful person can be described as FAT:

Faithful—doing what God desires
Available—willing to take time to grow
Teachable—desiring to learn

As president of the student body, a big football star, and the steady date of the head cheerleader, Todd looked like a pretty good candidate for being a disciple. He even expressed a desire to be involved. Yet I sensed that deep down he was not committed. He said he wanted to be discipled, but I kept putting him off. At that point he wasn't faithful, available, or teachable.

After he graduated he was left without the glory of football, without the applause of the student body, and without a girlfriend. (She dumped him.) He was humbled and began to desire God above all other things. At that point he became a FAT person—a faithful man.

THE POINT: RECRUIT ONLY THE FAITHFUL. Who would you like to recruit as a disciple? ________________. What makes that person faithful?

#6. PASS THE BATON. Look again at these words from 2 Timothy 2:2: "you," "me," "faithful men," and "others also."

These phrases speak of "passing the baton" from one spiritual generation to another. Paul's discipling stretched beyond Timothy to four generations of disciples:

Generation 1 — Paul
Generation 2 — Timothy
Generation 3 — Faithful men
Generation 4 — Others

Disciple-making includes having a perspective that extends beyond the person you are discipling to the rest of the world.

Here's how that can work: I discipled Bill while he was in college, and Bill led John to Christ. The summer after John's conversion, he and Bill went to the Soviet Union. Bill spent hours that summer discipling John. Bill and John went to the Moscow Baptist Church where they met Eugene, who was not a Christian but spoke some English. John took Eugene back to his room and talked to him about Christ. Eugene said he had already been considering Christianity, but he still wasn't ready to commit his life to Christ. Several months later John received a letter from Eugene telling him that he had become a Christian. He later received permission to emigrate. Eugene now lives in the United States and has a shortwave radio broadcast that reaches between 5 and 15 million people in the Soviet Union every week.

That is passing the baton.

Generation 1 — Barry
Generation 2 — Bill
Generation 3 — John
Generation 4 — Eugene
Generation 5 — Millions of others

THE POINT: PASS THE BATON BY DISCIPLING OTHERS. Think about the person whose name you wrote on page 114. Who are his or her friends?

____

____

Could one of these friends come to Christ and grow?
☐ Yes ☐ No Who? ____________________

Who are his other friends?

____

____

Could one of these come to Christ and grow? ☐ Yes
☐ No Who? ____________________

Get the point?

MAKING IT PERSONAL

Jesus has expressed His desire for us—"to go and make disciples" (Matthew 28:19). Then He tells us how to do that. What does He say? (Matthew 28:20)

____

____

In order to become a discipler of others you need some *practical steps* to begin:

STEP #1—PRAY. Ask the Lord:

- To make you an example—a model that younger students can follow.
- To convince you that this is the right way for you to invest your time. Then you will know this is a ministry He has led you to start.
- To show you how to get started.

STEP #2—DREAM. Dream about what could happen in your school and church as you disciple other students. Write out your dreams concerning how you want God to use you.

____

____

____

____

____

STEP #3—SELECT. "Whom should I disciple?" you ask. Follow these guidelines to find the right person.

1. Ask God to show you the right one. Often the person we would select is not the one God wants.
2. Determine what qualities you want in the person you will disciple. (See 1 Thessalonians 1 for some of the qualities you will want to look for.)
3. Keep your eyes open.
    - Find a person who is FAT—faithful, available, teachable.
    - Look in your youth group for a student who is two years younger than you.

    Get suggestions from your youth worker.
4. Involve him or her in a short-range project. Before you commit yourself, get him or her to help you do something that will require a sacrifice—such as helping you clean your car, helping your mom and dad with a project at home, or helping your youth minister with a project at church. That is one of the best ways to

tell if he is faithful.

5. Talk one-on-one about getting together for discipling. Set up a time to tell him about what you want to do.

STEP #4—COMMITMENT. When you talk to him:

1. Recruit him to the cause of Christ, not to going through a book. He will stay motivated that way.

2. Tell him how much this can mean to his life. Tell him what you have gotten out of it.

3. Tell him how much it will cost him. Look at Luke 9:23 with him. Explain what it has cost you.

4. Ask for a commitment. Get a copy of *Following Jesus* and go over page 7, "Purpose," and page 11, "Personal Commitment." Make sure he understands completely what is involved.

STEP #5—PREPARATION. Get your own copy of the *Following Jesus Leader's Guide.* Read and follow the instructions on pages 2-6. Take each suggestion seriously. The better you prepare, the better your discipleship time will go.

STEP #6— THE SESSION. Go through *Following Jesus* with him. You and your disciple should each have a copy. You, as the leader, should carefully follow the instructions of the *Leader's Guide.*

STEP #7—EVALUATION. Meet with your group leader or youth worker once every two weeks to talk about how things are going.

To complete this Bible study, memorize 2 Timothy 2:2.

ASSIGNMENT:

1. Have a time alone with God every day this week using the following Bible readings:
   Day 1: 2 Timothy 3:10-17
   Day 2: 2 Timothy 4:1-5
   Day 3: 2 Timothy 4:6-8
   Day 4: 2 Timothy 4:9-15
   Day 5: 2 Timothy 4:16-22

Day 6: Titus 1:1-4
Day 7: Titus 1:5-9

2. Complete *Bible study 10.*

3. Work on the group ministry project.

4. Get with your disciple and get everything prepared to begin *Following Jesus.*

NOTES

BIBLE STUDY

10

FROM HERE TO THERE

Developing a ministry strategy

How many more lunches are you going to eat in the cafeteria this year? ___ (Don't let your stomach lining go into spasms when you answer this.)

That represents the number of opportunities you have left for possible ministry before everyone scatters for the summer.

If you're at the end of the school year, think about how great it's going to be to eat your mom's lunch (peanut butter and jelly). Consider how many opportunities you will have to minister to the people around you this summer.

For nine weeks we have talked about ministering to others. Of all the things you have done during these nine weeks as a part of this group, what one thing have you enjoyed the most?

____

____

____

What is the most important insight you have gained about yourself?

____

____

What have you learned about ministering to others that is of the most value to you now?

____

____

By now you have a good grasp of what is involved in ministering to others. But how do you bring all of it into a focused plan that will cause you to have the maximum impact on the people around you?

Imagine you are in a room with a high ceiling. Tied to the ceiling is a sign that says "My Ministry." How are you going to get that sign? You can't climb through thin air to pick it up. You must use a ladder to reach it.

Your ladder is the "Practical Ministry Strategy." It will help you:

➫ GET AFTER IT. Don't waste God's time on things that don't matter. A Practical Ministry Strategy will help you to get after it.

➫ GET ON TOP OF IT. Some are run ragged going from one activity to the other. Don't lose perspective on what you are doing and why.

We find our Practical Ministry Strategy in Matthew 10. Read it and summarize Jesus' ministry strategy for His disciples.

The ladder to discovering your ministry will have these five rungs:

RUNG #1—OUR PURPOSE DRIVES OUR MINISTRY (Matthew 10:1, 5).

When we understand our life purpose, then we are motivated to minister to others. Jesus took three actions to help His disciples discover their purpose. He takes the same three actions with us. According to Matthew 10:1, 5a, Jesus called the disciples, gave them authority, and sent them.

To help His disciples discover their purpose . . . *Jesus "called His 12 disciples to Him."* He didn't call them to a job, a school, a cause, an activity, or a church. He called them "to Him." *They were called to a relationship with Jesus—to know Him, to love Him, and to please Him.*

We are called to the same relationship. Our purpose is to know, love, and please Jesus Christ. As a result of that relationship we begin to reflect Him in our relationships to others.

IN DISCOVERING OUR PURPOSE,
OUR MOTIVATION IS TO KNOW JESUS.

Jesus "gave them authority." In Acts we see the disciples preaching, healing, and carrying out other ministries. They were not doing this by their own strength, but through the authority of Jesus Christ. How did they get His authority?

Look at Matthew 28:18. How much authority did Jesus have? ________.

Hebrews 1:3 expresses how powerful Jesus' authority is. What does Jesus' powerful Word do? ____________

He gives us that same authority. What does Luke 10:19 tell us about our authority?

____

IN DISCOVERING OUR PURPOSE, OUR MINISTRY ABILITY COMES FROM HAVING JESUS' AUTHORITY.

"These Twelve Jesus sent out." The disciples, under Jesus' authority, went out into the world to minister to others. They, and those they influenced, "caused trouble all over the world" (Acts 17:5-7), proclaiming Jesus King.

Jesus sends us out with His authority to turn the world upside down.

IN DISCOVERING OUR PURPOSE,
OUR MISSION IS TO BE SENT OUT.

How can you live out your life purpose? Include these three points as you give specifics: To know and love Jesus Christ, to receive His authority, and to be sent out.

____

____

____

Now go back to *Following Jesus,* page 33, to see how you answered the same question before. How does that compare with your purpose now?

Knowing our purpose moves us to the next rung on the ladder to our ministry strategy.

RUNG #2—OUR PRIORITIES DECIDE OUR MINISTRY (Matthew 10:5-6).

Jesus tells the disciples what things are not the priorities of their ministry. What does He tell them not to do?

That narrows it down. Then Jesus tells them what to do. What does He say?

That focuses it in. Jesus looked across the world and saw millions of people. All of them needed Him, but He concentrated His disciples' efforts on one limited group of people (priority) to accomplish His ultimate purpose. You look at all the people in the world, the needs, and the ministry possibilities. You say, "I want to do it all, but where do I start?" Jesus says, "Narrow it down, focus it in."

In order to discover your ministry priority, consider:

- Your purpose.
- The needs of others that burden you.
- Your call.
- Your spiritual gift.

You will want to go back and review your responses in chapters 1, 2, and 5 in order to determine your ministry priority.

Now, describe in detail what you think your ministry priority is.

____

____

____

____

Go over this with your discipleship group leader.

Discovering our ministry priority moves us to the next rung.

RUNG #3—OUR PURSUIT OF GOALS DIRECTS OUR MINISTRY (Matthew 10:7-8). Jesus tells them, "As you go" (to the lost sheep of Israel). In other words, "As you move toward your ministry priority." Then He gives them five almost impossible goals (v. 8). What are they?

1.
2.
3.
4.
5.

As the disciples heard these goals, they probably said, "(Gulp!) Jesus, we've watched *You* pull this off, but good grief, there's no way *we* can do that. This scares us to death. Raise people from the dead? Give us a break." You would probably say that too.

Jesus might have said, "Let's review, men. Remember when we talked about authority? All of it belongs to Me. And I've given it to you. Because I do these things, you can do them. Freely you have received; freely give! If you possess Me and My power, then you have no right to keep it to yourself. You must give it away."

The disciples' reaction, and our reaction, happens because we're afraid to set big goals. We tend to settle for mediocrity because we set "man-sized goals" instead of "God-sized goals." But because we have Jesus' authority we can set God-sized goals. That's what is so neat about Jesus. He stretches us into the impossible—like raising people from the dead.

> SET BIG GOALS—SO BIG THAT IF GOD DOESN'T WORK, YOU'RE DOOMED TO FAILURE.

As you set goals for achieving your ministry priority, consider: Do they fit into your purpose? Do they reflect your ministry priority? Are they measurable and specific?

For example, one student wrote: My goals for reaching athletes (ministry priority) are:

1. To train six days a week so I can compete with excellence.
2. To develop a core group of five students to reach other athletes with me.
3. To encourage 15 athletes to come to my church this year to meet Christ and grow in Him.

Write out three faith goals that will take you toward your ministry priority.

Goal 1 ______________________________

Goal 2 ______________________________

Goal 3 ______________________________

Pursuing specific faith goals moves us to our next rung.

RUNG #4—OUR PLANS DEVELOP OUR MINISTRY (Matthew 10:9-39).

Jesus gives His disciples an eight-step plan to accomplish their ministry. Read the verses that go with each step.

STEP 1. Simplify your lifestyle (vv. 9-10).
STEP 2. Select your companions carefully (vv. 11-15).
STEP 3. Step out with shrewdness (vv. 16-17).
STEP 4. Speak in the Spirit (vv. 18-20).
STEP 5. Stand firm (vv. 21-25).
STEP 6. Set aside fear (vv. 26-31).

STEP 7. See that Jesus gets the glory (vv. 32-33).
STEP 8. Sacrifice everything (vv. 34-39).

As you read through verses 9-39 again, pick out the two steps that are the hardest for you to take. Explain why; then discuss how you can move forward.

1. ____

____

2. ____

____

In these verses, Jesus gives a positive plan of action for every difficult step. Plan three steps you will take to accomplish each of your goals. Include these in the Practical Ministry Plan on page 128. Fill it out and put it in your Spending Time Alone with God Notebook. Continue to update this every month.

By developing our ministry plan, we move up to the next ministry rung.

RUNG #5—OUR PAYOFF DEPENDS ON OUR MINISTRY (Matthew 10:40-42).

Jesus tells His disciples that they will receive a reward for their ministry. What does He say will cause His disciples to receive their reward? (v. 42)

____

____

William Barclay tells of Pizarro, the bold Spanish adventurer. He offered his little band a tremendous "choice between the known safety of Panama and the unknown splendor of Peru. He took his sword and traced a line with it in the sand. 'Friends and comrades,' he said, 'on that side are toil, hunger, nakedness, the drenching storm, desertion and death; on this side, ease and pleasure. There lies Peru with its riches; here, Panama and its poverty. Choose each man what best becomes him. For my part, I go south.' And he stepped across the line" (*The Daily Study Bible,* Harper & Row).

Jesus is inviting you to step across the line. To say it another way, He is inviting you to walk up the ladder of ministry. He didn't promise that it would be easy, but He did say the rewards would be great. Are you ready? Go for it!

MAKING IT PERSONAL

Complete this Bible study by memorizing Matthew 10:42.

ASSIGNMENT:

1. Have a time alone with God every day this week by using the following Bible readings:
   Day 1: Titus 1:10-16
   Day 2: Titus 2:1-5
   Day 3: Titus 2:6-10
   Day 4: Titus 2:11-15
   Day 5: Titus 3:1-7
   Day 6: Titus 3:8-11
   Day 7: Titus 3:12-15

   NOTE: Even though you have completed the Moving Toward Maturity series, you will want to continue to spend time alone with God and memorize Scripture every day. You can get additional *Time Alone with God Notebook Inserts* at your local Christian bookstore, from the publisher of this book, or from Reach Out Ministries.

2. Continue to minister to people in your cafeteria or wherever you find a need.

3. Carry out the "Practical Ministry Plan."

4. Continue to meet with your group to carry out the group project each week.

PRACTICAL MINISTRY PLAN

My Purpose in Life:

My Priority in Ministry:

My Pursuit of Ministry Goals and Ministry Plans:

GOAL	STEPS OF ACTION	DATE

1.
   a.
   b.
   c.
2.
   a.
   b.
   c.
3.
   a.
   b.
   c.

How do I see God rewarding me for my ministry?

Now Eternity

BIBLE MEMORY CARDS

ach memory verse on these cards is printed in the *New International Version* (NIV) and the *King James Version* (KJV). The verses orrespond with the Bible studies in this book. ut out the cards and packet along the olid black lines. Make the packet, insert the ards, and follow the instructions on the acket. ENJOY THE BENEFITS OF SCRIPTURE IEMORIZATION!

1. HARVEST FIELD Matthew 9:36-38 (NIV)
When He saw the crowds, He had compassion on them, because they were harassed and helpless, like sheep without a shepherd. Then He said to His disciples, "The harvest is plentiful but the workers are few. Ask the Lord of the harvest, therefore, to send out workers into His harvest field."

2. GO Jeremiah 1:7 (NIV)
But the Lord said to me, "Do not say, 'I am only a child.' You must go to everyone I send you to and say whatever I command you."

3. CALL TO ME Jeremiah 33:3 (NIV)
"Call to Me and I will answer you and tell you great and unsearchable things you do not know."

4. LOVE 1 Corinthians 13:4-8a (NIV)
Love is patient, love is kind. It does not envy, it does not boast, it is not proud. It is not rude, it is not self-seeking, it is not easily angered, it keeps no record of wrongs. Love does not delight in evil but rejoices with the truth. It always protects, always trusts, always hopes, always perseveres. Love never fails.

5. DIFFERENT GIFTS 1 Corinthians 12:4-6 (NIV)
There are different kinds of gifts, but the same Spirit. There are different kinds of service, but the same Lord. There are different kinds of working, but the same God works all of them in all men.

6. WASH FEET John 13:14-15 (NIV)
"Now that I, your Lord and Teacher, have washed your feet, you also should wash one another's feet. I have set you an example that you should do as I have done for you."

1. HARVEST FIELD *Matthew 9:36-38 (KJV)*
But when He saw the multitudes, He was moved with compassion on them, because they fainted and were scattered abroad, as sheep having no shepherd. Then saith He unto His disciples, "The harvest truly is plenteous, but the laborers are few. Pray ye therefore the Lord of the harvest, that He will send forth laborers into His harvest."

2. GO *Jeremiah 1:7 (KJV)*
But the Lord said unto me, "Say not, 'I am a child': for thou shalt go to all that I shall send thee, and whatsoever I command thee thou shalt speak."

3. CALL TO ME *Jeremiah 33:3 (KJV)*
"Call unto Me, and I will answer thee, and show thee great and mighty things, which thou knowest not."

4. LOVE *1 Corinthians 13:4-8a (KJV)*
Charity suffereth long, and is kind; charity envieth not; charity vaunteth not itself, is not puffed up, doth not behave itself unseemly, seeketh not her own, is not easily provoked, thinketh no evil; rejoiceth not in iniquity, but rejoiceth in the truth; beareth all things, believeth all things, hopeth all things, endureth all things. Charity never faileth.

5. DIFFERENT GIFTS *1 Corinthians 12:4-6 (KJV)*
Now there are diversities of gifts, but the same Spirit. And there are differences of administrations, but the same Lord. And there are diversities of operations, but it is the same God which worketh all in all.

6. WASH FEET *John 13:14-15 (KJV)*
"If I then, your Lord and Master, have washed your feet, ye also ought to wash one another's feet. For I have given you an example, that ye should do as I have done to you."

7. CHEERFUL GIVER 2 Corinthians 9:6-7 (NIV)
Remember this: Whoever sows sparingly will also reap sparingly, and whoever sows generously will also reap generously. Each man should give what he has decided in his heart to give, not reluctantly or under compulsion, for God loves a cheerful giver.

8. GREATEST COMMANDMENT Matthew 22:37-39 (NIV)
Jesus replied, " 'Love the Lord your God with all your heart and with all your soul and with all your mind.' This is the first and greatest commandment. And the second is like it: 'Love your neighbor as yourself.' "

9. TEACH OTHERS 2 Timothy 2:2 (NIV)
And the things you have heard Me say in the presence of many witnesses entrust to reliable men who will also be qualified to teach others.

10. REWARD Matthew 10:42 (NIV)
"And if anyone gives a cup of cold water to one of these little ones because he is My disciple, I tell you the truth, he will certainly not lose his reward."

PACKET FOR CARDS

- Cut out.
- Fold *in* on dotted lines.
- Tape short flap to back on outside edges.

INSTRUCTIONS:

- Always carry this packet with you.
- Memorize a verse a week.
- Daily review each verse you've learned.
- Have someone check your progress each week.
- Apply each verse to your daily life.

7. CHEERFUL GIVER 2 Corinthians 9:6-7 (KJV)
But this I say: He which soweth sparingly shall reap also sparingly; and he which soweth bountifully shall reap also bountifully. Every man according as he purposeth in his heart, so let him give; not grudgingly, or of necessity: for God loveth a cheerful giver.

8. GREATEST COMMANDMENT Matthew 22:37-39 (KJV)
Jesus said unto him, " 'Thou shalt love the Lord thy God with all thy heart, and with all thy soul, and with all thy mind.' This is the first and great commandment. And the second is like unto it: 'Thou shalt love thy neighbor as thyself.' "

9. TEACH OTHERS 2 Timothy 2:2 (KJV)
And the things that thou hast heard of Me among many witnesses, the same commit thou to faithful men, who shall be able to teach others also.

10. REWARD Matthew 10:42 (KJV)
"And whosoever shall give to drink unto one of these little ones a cup of cold water only in the name of a disciple, verily I say unto you, he shall in no wise lose his reward."

GROWING ON
Bible Memory Packet